True Scripture

The Bible stories you thought you knew

The Book of
Genesis

Sean O'Leary

True Scripture
The Bible Stories
You Thought You Knew

ABOUT TRUE SCRIPTURE

The purpose of *True Scripture* is to make the Bible easier to understand and enjoy for believers and non believers alike. Most people learn their Bible stories in Sunday School, confirmation class or weekly church service, which significantly limits the material to which they are exposed. While many take comfort in various inspirational passages, very few people indeed have read the entire book.

This situation has several explanations. For one thing, the Bible is not easy reading. Even newer translations written in more "modern" language tend to be long-winded, repetitious and puzzling. The chronology is hard to follow and passages are inserted seemingly at random. Some accounts contradict previous passages; other narrative segments are so confusing as to discourage any further reading.

Furthermore, priests, rabbis and ministers are tasked with expediting spiritual relationships with their God, not creating biblical scholars. In general, the clergy is unlikely to highlight such stories as Jephthah sacrificing his daughter on the altar to thank God for a military victory, Judah's daughter-in-law posing as a prostitute to trick him into fathering her children or Elisha summoning bears to kill forty-two children for the crime of mocking his bald pate.

True Scripture Point of View
True Scripture condenses what is written in the Bible into concise* and entertaining prose, including all of the surprising, amusing and sometimes disturbing details. The default standard is to take the Biblical text at face value and tell the story exactly as written. When this is impossible due to paradoxes, ambiguities or other glaring anomalies, *True Scripture* will generally address the problem directly and provide additional insight. With regard to painful components such as the genealogies, an explanation of the relevance of the material is provided, rather that an actual list of names.

In addition, easy to understand footnotes provide additional historical and linguistic perspectives for murky or ambiguous passages. As you read *True Scripture*, we invite you to follow along with your own Bible: nothing has been added or changed.

* Your total word savings over the King James Version is shown clearly at the beginning of each chapter.

The Book of Genesis

If you're looking for more Bible for your buck, there is no better value than the Book of Genesis. The first book of the Old Testament spans over half of the 4,100 year Biblical timeline, from Creation to the death of Joseph in Egypt in approximately 1675 B.C. That's over 2300 total years! In Genesis, you will consider key questions such as:

- After God creates Man, why does He create Man again (page 6)?
- Who are the mysterious giants known as Nephilim (page 10)?
- Why does Noah sacrifice all the animals after saving them (page 12)?
- Who are the imaginary helpers to whom God speaks on several occasions early in Genesis (page 15)?
- Why couldn't God beat Jacob in a wrestling match (page 42)?
- What was the ancient Hebrew concept of Hell (page 48)?
- What was Judah's relationship with his daughter-in-law (page 50)?
- How many Hebrew tribes are there supposed to be (page 60)?
- Why were Jacob and Joseph mummified in Egypt (page 64)?

These stories and more are all found in the amazing *Book of Genesis*.

Key Genesis Locations

1. Garden of Eden: The precise setting and acreage of the garden are unknown but many believe it is in the vicinity of the location shown on the map. According to the text, the Tree of Life should still be there (Gen. 3).

2. Noah's Ark: Does not land on Mount Ararat but in a region known as the Mountains of Ararat. Today, this location is somewhere in the frontier area of modern Turkey and Armenia (Gen. 6-9).

3. Ur of the Chaldees (Sumer): A capital of the ancient Sumerian civilization, this location is traditionally (Jewish) understood to be the homeland of Abram/Abraham, the first Patriarch (Gen. 11).

4. Haran (also Padan-aram): Abram's father establishes a new family base here. Isaac and Jacob return here to get brides (Gen. 11).

5. Caanan / Promised Land: The three Patriarchs and their clan spend much of Genesis here. God promises this land to Abraham, Isaac and Jacob a total of thirteen times in Genesis.

6. Goshen (also Rameses): Genesis ends in this fertile area on the eastern Nile Delta. Joseph settles Jacob here and it becomes the starting point for the Exodus hundreds of years later.

Beth-El (Bethel): A popular altar building destination for Abraham (Gen. 12) and his offspring.

Hebron/Tree of Mamre: South of Jeru-Salem in the Judean hills. Abraham builds an altar and purchases a cave here, where Sarah and the big three Patriarchs will eventually be buried (Gen. 13).

Beersheba/Gerar: Desert area of south central Canaan, 13 Km southeast of Gaza. Abraham does his second "she's my sister" bit here and banishes his concubine and son in the wilderness of Beersheba (Gen. 12 / Gen. 16).

Shechem: Site of Abraham's first altar (Gen.11) and the great Oak Tree at Moreah. Also where Jacob's sons initiate a heinous mass circumcision and massacre (Gen. 33).

Seir: Another name for Edom, a wasteland to the south and Esau's home (Gen 35).

Key Places and Event Locations In the Book of Genesis

Only Noah saw it coming
Forty days and forty nights
Took his sons and daughters* with him.
Yeah, they were the Israelites!**

The Hooters
All You Zombies
1982

* Incorrect. Noah did not take his daughters
** Incorrect. There will be no Israelites for at least half a millenium after the Flood.

Genesis 1

*God creates the Heavens, Earth, upper and lower waters, light sources,
living things and Mankind, all in six days.*

[KJV 787] TSB 402: *Your Savings 385*

God[1a] abruptly creates the heavens and the earth, but they are formless and dark. He solves the darkness problem by creating Light. He examines the Light and is satisfied with it, so he divides it from the Darkness and names it Day. The Darkness is designated as Night. A good first day's work.

Next day, God creates a large solid structure to divide the upper waters from the lower waters. He calls this firmament Heaven.[1b]

The third day is one of God's most productive. First he gathers the waters together to make the seas. That undertaking exposes some dry land and provides somewhere to stand. He calls this dry area Earth and the gathered waters Seas. Here He plants grass, herb yielding seeds and fruit trees.

Next day, he places a greater light, a lesser light and stars in the Heavens to illuminate the Earth. The purpose, he explains, is not only to divide Day from Night, but also to indicate signs, seasons, days and years.

On the fifth day, he compels the lower waters to produce living, moving creatures, along with birds to fly above the Earth. He singles out whales in a separate act of creation, possibly due to their size. He instructs all of these sea creatures to begin reproducing.

At the beginning of the key sixth day, God is ready to populate the land, which he fills with cattle, creeping things and beasts. He is so pleased with this effort that he decides to make Man. He causes consternation for future scholars by describing this new inhabitant of the Earth as being in "our" image and "our" likeness.[1c] God does not explain to whom he is speaking but in a sense he is speaking to himself. He creates both male and female types of Man, tells them to get busy and have kids and also to rule over everything else He has made.

So after six days of work, we are left with a brand new universe that is somewhat circumscribed but relatively straightforward. In the center are the Heavens, which include two lights and an unspecified number of stars. Above Heaven, which is described as a vault or firmament, are the upper waters remaining from the first day's work. Below Heaven is the dry land called Earth, and also the Seas, which were formed from the lower waters. The seas, land and sky are populated with living creatures and also Man, male and female.

GENESIS 1 NOTES:

Date: ~ 4,000 B.C.

1a. "God" is given several names in the original Hebrew texts, including the early Elohim (El) and Jahweh (JHWH). We will provide additional comment on God's names when appropriate, but the running narrative will refer to the Old Testament deity either as *God* or *the Lord*.

1b. The exact meaning of the word firmament in Gen. 1 continues to be debated from both a theological and linguistic point of view.

1c. For those of a monotheistic persuasion, the use of the first person plural ("us") by the creator God may be puzzling. God is addressing other entities who look like He does - but who are they? One clue is that the most ancient Hebrew deity Elohim or El began his career as one of many local gods in the region east of the Mediterranean Sea. Furthermore, the word Elohim is a masculine *plural* and also ambiguous, suggesting the godhead was accompanied by divine helpers who are either angels or similar to angels. In the New Testament, the Christian version of the god of Genesis echoes and refines this plurality by taking the form of the Trinity.

The word "El" is also the standard term for "god" in other related Semitic languages including Ugaritic, the ancient Canaanite language.

GENESIS 2 NOTES:

2a. Bible literalists have expended a great deal of effort working up arguments explaining why Gen. 2 does not contradict Gen. 1. But Gen. 2 does contradict Gen. 1 and does so plainly and unequivocally.

In Gen. 1, God creates animals and birds on the fifth day, then creates Man on the sixth day. To emphasize this point, He explicitly makes Man in the likeness of Himself (and his angels) and gives him dominion over the fish / fowl / cattle already created. Yet in Gen.2, after resting on the seventh day, God notices that nothing is growing and there is no one to till the ground. It is for this clearly stated reason that God creates (male) Man (again) and places him in the Garden of Eden. Again unambiguously, it is only then that God decides to create animals - specifically to help Man. This is exactly the reverse order of that found in the previous chapter, in which all non-human living things are created, and then Man and Woman.

True Scripture refers to these lapses as "it's-not-you…it's-the-Bible" scenarios. Clergy are generally not forthcoming about such contradictions, leaving the reader to doubt their own ability to understand the holy word. Stop worrying: sometimes the holy word is simply flawed.

2b. This is an early example of God making a threat and not following through.

Genesis 2

After resting on the seventh day, God begins to create living things all over again, but in a different order than the first time.

[KJV 632] TSB 483: *Your Savings 149*

As the second chapter opens, God spends the seventh day resting from all this work and he enjoys his day off so much that he blesses his creation. But it turns out (as is so often the case) that the work is not truly complete.[2a] For one thing, we are told that nothing is growing yet because God has not sent the rain. Instead, the land is temporarily watered by a mist which (judging from the poor agricultural results) is inadequate as irrigation.

Perhaps more alarming is the news that even though God and his friends made Man on the sixth day, there are now no men to till the earth. We proceed not knowing what happened to the Man folk who had been previously created. Whatever the explanation, God forms Man again from dust and blows breath into his nostrils, causing the Man to be alive. He situates the newly formed Man in a garden he has planted "eastward in Eden."

In addition to decorative and fruit bearing trees, God has also planted two other trees in the garden: the *Tree of Life*, and the *Tree of the Knowledge of Good and Evil*. To supplement the ineffective mist, a river provides irrigation for the garden. After emerging from the garden, this same river splits into four parts: the Pison, the Gihon (which flows to Ethiopia), the Hiddekel (which goes to Assyria and is understood to be the Tigris) and the Euphrates.

God puts the Man he has just created into the garden and instructs him to take care of this patch of paradise, but not to eat of the fruit of the Tree of Good and Evil. The penalty for disobedience is death.[2b] There are no instructions regarding the Tree of Life.

God realizes the Man needs a helper, and He decides to make him a companion to help with the gardening. This turns out to be more complicated than originally believed. First, God tries forming every beast of the field "out of the ground" and every fowl of the air (even though they were already created in Gen.1). At this point, the Man's name is casually revealed to be Adam, and Adam is instructed to name all the beasts and birds. This he does, but none of them seem suitable to be his helper. What to do? We gotta get you a woman!

After putting Adam to sleep, God takes one of his ribs, from which he fashions his helper. Adam has grown so adept at naming cattle and birds, that he confidently names his new helper Woman *"because she was taken out of Man."* [KJV]

It is noted here that a man shall leave his father and his mother and shall cleave unto his wife and they shall be one flesh, and also that Adam and Woman were not embarrassed, even though they were naked. This is not yet a problem as Woman still does not have a name.

Genesis 3

A long term moral trend is set for humankind, as the serpent talks Eve into some forbidden behavior; she in turn talks Adam into a major error that causes consternation for the next 6,000 years plus.

[KJV 695] TSB 475: *Your Savings 220*

As Gen. 3 opens, everything is going well in the Garden until we meet the serpent, who begins working on Woman.[3a] He insists Adam and Woman will not die if they eat the fruit of the Knowledge of Good and Evil tree, but will rather become like God.[3b] Woman quickly sees that this particular fruit not only bestows wisdom, but looks tasty as well. She eats some and gives some to Adam, who also tries a bite. As predicted, the naughty pair immediately acquire wisdom, which manifests itself instantly as an understanding of the challenges of nakedness. Now that they are wise, the first thing Adam and Woman do is make themselves aprons out of fig leaves. Even though they are wearing strategic fig fashions, when they hear God's voice in the garden they hide from him. Adam tells God he is hiding because he is naked, which arouses God's suspicions. When asked about eating from the Tree of the Knowledge of Good and Evil, Adam cracks instantly and blames Woman for giving him the fruit. She in turn blames the serpent.

God dispenses justice as follows: The snake has to crawl and eat dust from now on, plus he is accursed and will be enemies with the Woman and her descendants. They will kick him whenever they get a chance. As for the Woman, she will be ruled by her husband, and equally unpleasant, childbirth is going to be quite painful. As for Adam, his punishment for listening to the Woman is that he is going to have to work for living from now on. The soil is not going to give up food so easily in the future: farming just got a lot harder, my Man. God isn't done yet, because when all of this travail is over, Adam and Woman will have to return to the ground: *"for out of it wast thou taken: for dust thou art, and unto dust shalt thou return."* [KJV]

After this fiasco, Adam decides he may as well give Woman a name. He selects "Eve", which connotes one who will be the mother of everyone else. God replaces the fig leaves with some decent threads made out of animal skin.

God once again addresses his imaginary angel friends regarding the new developments with Adam and Eve. He is concerned that they have already become "like one of us" because of the recent wisdom acquisition.[3c] God shares an even greater concern with his presumably divine colleagues: what if Adam and Eve also eat from the Tree of Life and become immortal?

So Adam and Eve are banished from the Garden of Eden before they can achieve eternal life. A cherubim is placed at the east entry of the garden to prevent re-entry and a flaming sword swings back and forth to discourage dining at the Tree of Life.

GENESIS 3 NOTES:

3a. Some wags have pointed out that Eve can't be blamed for disobeying God because she didn't yet have the knowledge of good and evil, sort of a reverse Catch 22. But even if they are right, it's too late to take Elohim to court.

3b. The Serpent, it turns out, has his facts straight.

3c. The nature of "us" once again is not specified. In a historical context, the mythology of the surrounding peoples described a pre-Homeric world in which deities and humans intermingled and interbred.

GENESIS 4 NOTES:

4a. The Hebrew word for "sin" can also mean "sin-offering". This aspect of the Cain/Abel story marks the beginning of an obsession with burnt offerings (and particularly animal fat) in Old Testament chronicles, and reveals the objectives of the priest/scribe class who composed these documents. As we continue, note the many key events that focus upon animal (and occasionally human) sacrifice.

4b. Cain was probably over reacting, as the population of Earth was back down to three with his brother gone to meet his maker. Anyone else Cain encountered in the world would be his younger siblings and we have no news of them having been born yet, so where is the problem.

4c. Cain's wife had to be either an unnamed sister, or - a stretch - a descendant of his brother Seth, which would make her his niece. The latter interpretation can be found in Mormon Founder Joseph Smith's version of the Bible...no surprise.

4d. This Enoch is not the same person as Noah's great grandfather nor is he the mythological subject of *1 Enoch*, an apocryphal scripture excluded from official Jewish and Catholic canon. It includes the *Book of Watchers*, a rollicking good fantasy tale of fallen angels, enchantments and giants.

4e. Particularly in the book of Genesis, various out of context "interludes" are inserted into the storyline. These narrative insertions sometimes attempt to explain the origins and movements of the Earth's peoples. This one contains echoes of the Atlantis myth. As we will also see, there is often some political agenda embedded into the account. Some of these agendas continue to operate in modern times.

Genesis 4

Cain and Abel are born and 25% of the human population is wiped out.

[KJV 632] TSB 525: *Your Savings 107*

Adam and Eve begin breeding. Eve gives birth to Cain and comments: *"With God's help I have gotten a man."* [KJV] Next comes Abel. Cain decides to be a farmer and Abel decides to be sheep herder, which pretty much covered the available career options at the time.

The trouble begins when the brothers bring offerings to God. Cain brings farm goods and Abel brings the firstborn lamb's fat. God expresses pleasure with Abel's offering but is not impressed with that of Cain. The Lord sees that Cain is disappointed, but tells him he will be accepted if he does what is right. Further, if Cain's offering has been rejected, then sin is clearly at his door and must be overcome.[4a]

Cain evidently misses God's point, because his reaction is to take Abel out in the field and kill him. When God asks Cain where Abel is, Cain famously replies *"I know not: Am I my brother's keeper?"* [KJV] God of course knows what has happened because Abel's blood has been crying out to him from the ground. Since He is also omniscient, the assumption here is that He is asking Cain a more or less rhetorical question.

He banishes Cain from the soil and condemns him to wandering the earth. When Cain complains, God marks him so that no one will kill him on account of the fact he is a restless wanderer.[4b] He goes to live in the land of Nod, which is East of Eden. Of the four humans who have populated the Earth thus far, three have messed up royally and one is dead.

A sadder but wiser man, Cain gets together with his wife[4c] (who has appeared from nowhere) and conceives a son, Enoch.[4d] He is so happy he builds a city, which he names after his son. Enoch begins breeding and his male descendants are: Irad, who begat Mehujael who begat Methusael who begat Lamech, the next interesting person in the Bible.

The Lamech interlude interjected here concerns the legendary origins of certain trades or occupations.[4e] By his wife Adah he has two sons, Jabal and Jubal. The former is the father of all future herders who live in tents and the latter is the father of those who play the harp and flute. By his other wife Zillah, Lamach produces Tubalcain, who is the original teacher of everyone who works in brass and iron going forward.

Suddenly, Lamech launches an out of context rant, telling his wives that he has slain a young man in self-defense, but that he will be avenged seventy-seven fold if someone kills him because of the crime. He further explains that anyone who might have killed Cain, by contrast, would only be avenged sevenfold. This is the last we hear directly of Cain's progeny.

Adam and Eve breed again and produce another son, the younger brother of the recently deceased Abel and his brother Cain. As noted by Eve, the name Seth means he has been provided by God as replacement for Abel. Seth fathers Enosh with an unnamed wife and we are further informed that men began to call upon the name of the Lord at about this time.

Genesis 5

A quick romp through 1,000 years of Adam's descendants.[5a]

[KJV 504] TSB 183: *Your Savings 321*

This is the material in the Biblical narrative that most people skip right over: the genealogies. Luckily, *True Scripture* is committed to providing readers with the significance and context of the genealogies, without having to actually struggle through them. As we continue with the generations of Adam, we are not going to name every descendant. However, the reader should be aware that the primary narrative function of Gen. 5 is to set up the Flood story.

After a brief recapitulation of the Creation, we discover that Adam was one hundred-thirty years of age when he fathered Seth, after which he lived eight hundred years, for a grand total of nine-hundred thirty years.[5b]

Adam's third son Seth begets Enosh, and then seven more generations follow until we arrive at Noah, son of Lamech (a different Lamech than Cain's descendant). Noah has three sons: Shem, Ham and Japheth. For reasons that will become obvious, everyone on the planet today is necessarily descended from these three individuals. Slightly more than one thousand years have elapsed since the unfortunate incident in the Garden of Eden.

Noah sacrifices every clean animal and the aroma causes God to issue a limited guarantee!

5a. These lengthy accountings of who begat whom are undoubtedly responsible for the inclination of millions of people to skip over them. There is no question these lists are mind-numbing, but they are also critical to understanding many of the key links and prophecies throughout the Bible, especially prophecies about David and Jesus. In fact, one of the more surprising results of following the genealogies is the discovery of skeletons in the closets of Jesus' forebears. The genealogies also serve to legitimize the claim to the Promised Land.

5b. The Evangelical Christian "Young Earth" scenario is based on the belief that everything written in the Bible is literally true. It postulates a planet that is about 6,000 years old, meaning Adam was alive for approximately 17% of the elapsed time since Creation Day One.

GENESIS 6 NOTES:

Date: ~ 2,950 B.C. - 2,350 B.C.

6a. The language is tricky here: the "sons of God" are generally taken to be the sons of "good" Seth, while the daughters of men are taken to be the offspring of "bad" Cain. As such, these women are nice looking, but lacking in moral fiber. There is further confusion concerning the relationship among Seth's offspring and Elohim's composite nature. Some angels also seem to fancy the daughters of men.

6b. This and subsequent mentions of *Nephilim* incorporate non-Hebrew ancient mythologies as well as the extra-biblical Book of *1 Enoch* and *Book of Jubilees*. These mysterious beings are the fallen angels or Watchers who came to earth and mated with humans, creating half-angel, half human beings described as giants or Nephilim. Gen. 6:4 indicates the Niphilim survived the Flood and later in the Bible we encounter Niphilim and other giants such as Gog and Magog. Muslim scholar Javid Ahmed Ghamidi contends that Gog and Magog are the descendents of Noah's son Japhtheh. That's right: Chariots of the Gods.

6c. No sense that God feels any responsibility for the quality of his creative work.

6d. Generally understood to be cypress.

6e. This had to be emotionally devastating for Noah, as some simple arithmetic reveals that such well known characters as the famously long-lived Methuselah (Noah's grandfather) would have drowned in the flood. We can only conclude that Noah's forebears were also wicked, as well as his daughters. Sorry Grandpa! How long can you tread water?

6f. This passages is important: *"And of every living thing of all flesh, two of every sort shalt thou bring into the ark, to keep them alive with thee; they shall be male and female."* [KJV]

6g. What the animals and birds did to deserve their fate, as compared to fish, is unclear, but it could simply be a matter of expediency.

Genesis 6

God gives mankind 120 years to straighten out, but mankind does not . As a result, the Lord gets ready to destroy the world with a flood; He issues instructions to Noah.

[KJV 579] TSB 384: *Your Savings 195*

In this chapter, God becomes disillusioned with mankind. The sons of God become interested in the daughters of men and take them as mates indiscriminately.[6a] God indicates he is not going to put up with this forever, but gives them a hundred twenty years to reform - more than reasonable.

Among the offspring of the new generation are the Nephilim, a race of mighty giants.[6b] Having noted this, the story continues to remark upon the evil of man's ways as God is having second thoughts about creating them.[6c] He contemplates destroying Man, animals, creatures that move along the ground and birds of the air. As far as we know, he remains satisfied with the Heavens, Earth, fish and Noah.

God is OK with Noah because he is righteous and walks with the Lord, but He informs Noah he is going to destroy the world because of its violence and wickedness. Noah is instructed to build an Ark (which amounts to a large floating box) out of gopher wood.[6d] He is told the Ark should be 450 feet long, 75 feet wide and 45 feet high, contain many rooms and be sealed with tar or pitch. It should have a roof, a door and lower, middle and upper decks.

The reason for all this carpentry is that God has now narrowed his methods of destruction and is going to go with a flood. Everything will perish except Noah and part of his family. In addition to his wife, Noah is told to bring aboard his sons and their wives. Sadly, Noah's daughters are not on the list of people and creatures to be saved. Neither are his parents and grandparents.[6e]

In Genesis 6:19 Noah is commanded to bring aboard the male and female of all living creatures for the purpose of keeping them alive.[6f] God expands this command: Two of every kind of bird, of every kind of animal and of every kind of creature that moves along the ground. No fish are specified, which is unremarkable: this is going to be a flood after all and shouldn't worry fish or whales.[6g]

God specifies that these species will come to Noah, so that the Ark builder doesn't have to scour Earth looking for them when he could be working on the Ark. God also reminds Noah to take enough food for everyone.

Genesis 7

God changes his instructions about counting the animals, then everyone who qualifies boards the Ark. Noah follows God's original directive, and the springs of the deep burst forth!

[KJV 584] TSB 448: *Your Savings 136*

When Noah has accomplished all this (no time frame is indicated in the text), God tells him to get aboard the Ark. But now, after having explicitly and clearly told Noah to bring aboard two of every species, God tells Noah to take with him *seven* pairs of every clean animal, *seven* pairs of every bird and *two* of every unclean animal.[7a]

We're going to pause for another "it's-not-you...it's-the-Bible" break. You have probably noticed that God has now changed his instructions regarding the quantities of animals, birds etc. to be taken aboard the Ark. First, it was one pair each (two by two), but now it's seven pairs each. And that is exactly what it says in any mainstream version of the Bible. Over the years, literalist Bible scholars (those who believe every word in the Bible is true as dictated by God and written down by Moses) have generated an enormous amount of pretzel logic explaining why the passage that says to take seven pairs of each animal does not contradict the passage (four verses previously) that says to take one pair of each animal. But it does indeed contradict it. Usually, this sort of discussion will be found in the foot notes, but *True Scripture* wants you to understand that this is a common occurrence in the Bible. Check your own Bible from Gen. 6:20 to 7:3 to form your own opinion. See? It's not you.[7b]

As we continue, God warns Noah that the rains will start in seven days and wipe out every living thing from upon the Earth. As Noah and the specified members of his family board, Noah is still a vital middle aged man of only six hundred years. Whatever God's previous instructions in Gen. 7:3, the animals that board the Ark in Gen. 7:8 are once again in pairs, both clean and unclean. This will be important in about a year.

On the seventeenth day of the seventh month, Noah, Shem, Ham and Japheth et al enter the Ark as the floodgates of heaven open[7c], and the *"springs of the great deep burst forth."* [KJV] The single pairs of every kind of animal are explicitly mentioned once again as God shuts the door.

It rains for forty days and nights and the flood covers all the mountains to a depth of twenty feet, luckily lifting the Ark on the surface of the waters. Every living thing on the Earth that wasn't already on the Ark is destroyed. The flood lasts for a hundred fifty days.

GENESIS 7 NOTES:

7a. Regarding clean and unclean animals: Children in Sunday School have been known to wonder aloud why Noah didn't just give the unclean animals a bath. Many adults know that the reference here is to future Jewish dietary laws dictated to Moses, but God will not inform mankind what animals are clean and unclean until Leviticus, more than a thousand years in the future. Remember: Noah wasn't Jewish.

7b. Most scholars believe this and other sections of the Old Testament were written by multiple sources, which were later redacted (edited) together. The Noah cycle reads as if two different or more versions were cobbled together, because that's what essentially happened.

A number of parallel Mesopotamian flood myths have been unearthed over the years, describing flood water sources ranging from "windows of heaven" to the "fountains of the deep". The closest to the Biblical version is a 7th century B.C. Babylonian copy of the *Epic of Gilgamesh* (more or less, the Hercules of the Fertile Crescent). The hero Gilgamesh meets the immortal man Utnapishtim, who explains that the god Ea warned him to build a huge vessel in which to save himself, family, friends and animals. When the Hebrews spend quality time in Babylon during the sixth century (Jeremiah, 2 Kings) the *Epic of Gilgamesh* would have been widely available.

7c. We had previously noted that Noah and his family had already boarded the Ark a week ago. This is another result of parallel versions edited together..

GENESIS 8 NOTES:

8a. The Bible does not refer to Mt. Ararat but rather to the mountains of the Land of Ararat. This territory is located in the modern nations of Turkey and Armenia (see page 4). Mount Masis on the border of Turkey and Armenia was renamed Mt. Ararat in order to correspond to Muslim versions of the flood story. This information should be taken into consideration by those who continue to search for the remnants of the wooden Ark 4,350 years later.

8b. The sacrifice of "every" animal and bird carries with it all kinds of uncomfortable implications, not the least of which is: Why did Noah save the poor beasts if he was just going to kill and grill them? The confusion between the "two by two" and "seven by seven" versions becomes much more important in this context, as does God's clear indication that an important part of the mission is to save the animals. If Noah brought along only pairs, then the sacrifice of every clean animal or even one of each pair would finish the job the Flood started. It also brings up an awkward question: where did modern clean animals come from? Literalists have answers for all these questions, but they are agonizing to read. One theory is that the animals all got pregnant on the Ark and had baby animals. Presumably Noah let these babies off the hook. *True Scripture* is tasked with reporting only what the Bible says, but if we were to jump into this debate we would point out that giraffes have a gestation period of fifteen months. So the fact that we have giraffes in the modern world is another biblical miracle.

8c. It is the savory smoke from the sacrificial barbecue that triggers God's self-imposed moratorium on ground cursing, despite the human species' inherent wickedness. There will be other indications in Genesis that God is willing to overlook moral lapses if the sacrifices are up to snuff.

Genesis 8

Noah and all remaining living things disembark. Noah sacrifices all the clean animals and the fragrance of their burning carcasses pleases God so much that he makes a major commitment to humanity.

[KJV 586] TSB 394: *Your Savings 192*

The Bible doesn't tell us what God was doing during the five or so months the world was covered with water, only that He "remembers" Noah after the hundred fiftieth day. Once He recalls the flood situation, He sends a wind, which causes the waters to recede enough for the Ark to come to rest on the mountains of Ararat.[8a] The waters continue to abate for another two and a half months, which brings us to the first day of the tenth month. At this point, the tops of mountains began to appear.

Forty more days after that, Noah decides "why not open the window?" and sends out a raven. The bird flies back and forth until the water dries up. After some time, Noah also sends out a dove, but the dove has to return because it has no dry place to land. Noah waits a week and sends the dove again and this time it returns with an olive leaf in its mouth. Another week later, he sends the dove again, and it doesn't come back. Did its mate, the only other dove left on Earth, go find it? We are not told.

Ten and a half months after the flood began, Noah removes the cover of the Ark to see that the ground is relatively dry. But it isn't until two months later that the ground is completely dry and God tells Noah it's time to leave the Ark. In case Noah is unsure about the next step, God prompts him to offload the animals and birds. He makes a point of reminding Noah that the purpose of the trip was in large part to allow these creatures to multiply, be fruitful and increase in number. God's statement acquires ironic relevance as we near the end of the Noah/Flood segment because it makes Noah's decision to sacrifice "every clean beast" all the more puzzling:

And Noah builded an altar unto the LORD; and took of every clean beast, and of every clean fowl, and offered burnt offerings on the altar.[8b] And the LORD smelled a sweet savour; and the LORD said in his heart, I will not again curse the ground any more for man's sake; for the imagination of man's heart is evil from his youth; neither will I again smite any more every thing living, as I have done.[8c] [KJV]

Genesis 9

In this chapter, God shows early signs of a tendency to repeat himself, and also what seems to be an obsession with humanity's eating habits. Ham messes things up for his descendants.

[KJV 658] TSB 533: *Your Savings 125*

As the chapter opens, God blesses Noah, and commands the remnants of humankind to *"Be fruitful, and multiply, and replenish the earth."* [9a] [KJV]

In a series of admonitions, God gives Noah and his sons dominion over the beasts, which will now live in fear and dread of mankind. The beasts are given to man as food, more or less as a supplement to the vegetation already provided. However, just to show he isn't insensitive to animal rights, God forbids cooking or eating animals while they are still alive. Furthermore, the blood of the animal is not to be eaten.

While still on the subject of blood, God forbids the taking of another man's life and stipulates death as punishment for murder. Man will shed the blood of any other man who sheds blood, because man is made in God's image. This explains why killing a man is a heinous crime. [9b]

After God repeats several of his directives regarding mankind's responsibility to breed, he establishes a covenant with Noah, the flood survivors and all living things. He promised that *a flood* will never again destroy all life on Earth. [9c] As a sign, God sets his bow in the clouds. This statement has generally been interpreted to mean a rainbow, especially in light of its association with wet weather. God indicates the rainbow will also serve as a reminder to Himself of his promise, whenever He is creating rainstorms, that He should not let things get out of hand. The Lord goes on to reference the rainbow several times. [9d]

Once He gets past the rainbow, God notes more or less in passing that everyone on Earth will be descended from Shem, Ham and Japheth. Ham is singled out early as the father of Canaan, and soon we will see why.

The next thing we know, Noah is planting a vineyard, making wine and getting drunk. So drunk, in fact that he passes out naked in his tent. Ham goes in and sees him naked, which turns out to be a serious moral blunder of some sort. [9e] We are reminded that Ham, the youngest, is the father of Canaan, and therefore the Canaanites, and now we get a preview as to why the Canaanites are on shaky ground with God from this point on.

The good sons Shem and Japheth, who explicitly are *not* the fathers of Canaanites, manage to cover up Dad without peeking at his nakedness. When Noah finds out what Ham has done, he curses the Canaanites that are in the early stages of becoming Ham's descendants. He indicates that the Canaanites should be the slaves of their brothers. [9f] In fact, they should specifically be the slaves of Shem. He also hopes that Japheth will extend his territory. While this is a nice sentiment, it should be noted that there is nothing *but* territory at this point in history, so extending it should be a slam dunk.

Noah then enjoys another three hundred fifty years, which would place his death at about 2000 B.C. [9g] The first ten generations of humankind have taken up about one third of Biblical history.

GENESIS 9 NOTES:

Date: ~ 2,350 - 2,000 B.C.

9a. This is one commandment human kind took seriously.

9b. Unless you are God.

9c. An important but often overlooked detail is that God promises not to destroy the world by flood. *He does not promise not to destroy the world.*

9d. One of the advantages of being God is that no one says, "Right, you already mentioned that."

9e. Considering some of the behavioral lapses to come, Ham's inadvertent act seems mild. God has issued a few guidelines at this point, but "make sure not to see your Dad naked" is not among them. Ham's *crime* was seeing his Dad naked, but his *mistake* was telling his brothers. This is an unfortunate oversight for Ham's descendants, the Canaanites. They will eventually become the accursed Palestinians, still paying for Ham's crime.

9f. This will all come in handy when the Hebrews get to the Promised Land and find it already full of Canaanites.

9g. In terms of regional history, the flood would have taken place during Egypt's Old Kingdom, and Noah's death would approximately coincide with the beginnings of the Middle Kingdom. In Mesopotamia (Syria/Iraq), the sophisticated city states of the Tigris - Euphrates valley were a thousand years along in the development of urban civilization. To the southeast, the technologically advanced Indus Valley Civilization had also been flourishing for six hundred years.

GENESIS 10 NOTES:

10a. Anthropologically speaking, this mythology parallels stories of contemporaneous accounts of Atlantis. The early Greeks worshipped Japheth as Iapetos, or Iapetus, whom they regarded as the son of heaven and earth, the father of many nations. In the ancient Sanskrit Vedas of India, he is remembered as Pra-Japati, the sun and Lord of Creation. As time went by, Japheth's name was further corrupted, being assimilated into the Roman pantheon as Iupater, and possibly Jupiter. Both the early Irish Celts and the ancient Britons traced the descent of their royal houses from Japheth. Not the Chosen People, but not too shabby either.

10b. Many scholars think Nimrod has been conflated with the archetypal Sumerian hero Gilgamesh. Nimrod, along with other characters and events in this chapter are also found in extra-biblical traditions. His name has been associated with the Tower of Babel, implying he was a rebel against the Lord.

Genesis 10

Noah's three sons' descendants and their whereabouts.

[KJV 495] TSB 362: *Your Savings 133*

We now encounter another genealogy, this one based on the three sons of Noah. We are not going to list all of these people, but will rather note the various races, peoples or nations attributed to specific Noah offspring. Of Japheth's descendants, we have minimal commentary with the exception of his son Javan, whose descendants became the seafaring peoples that spread out to various lands. Japheth is often considered to be the father of the Indo-European peoples.[10a]

While Japheth's descendants are somewhat neglected, Ham's lineage is described in detail. Already identified as a bad egg (but not yet forbidden by kosher law) Ham has four sons, all of whom turn out to be forebears of undesirable races. The previously mentioned Canaan is father to the people who are already living in the Promised Land when God gives it away. Cush is father to the Ethiopian people, and the other two are Egyptians and Libyans, more or less. There is some foreshadowing here, such as the aside that Cush is grandfather of the warrior-hero Nimrod. Gen. 10 goes on to describe Nimrod's founding of Babylon, Nineveh and other cities in the Fertile Crescent.[10b] This reference places his descendants in eastern Mesopotamia as well as the area of the Zagros mountains.

The Philistines, villains of later Bible stories including the classic Samson and David confrontations, are also slotted as descendants of Ham/Cush. No surprise there. The lack of moral fiber that caused Ham to look upon Noah's nakedness was clearly passed down in his DNA to these prototypical enemies of the Israelites. Also descended from Canaan are the Hittites (from his son Heth), Jebusites and Amorites, all reprehensible tribes who will eventually try to prevent God's Chosen People from moving in after their forty year trip from Egypt (Exodus). The eventual borders of Canaan are described as reaching from Sidon toward Gerar as far as Gaza, and then toward Sodom and Gomorrah.

It is from middle brother Shem that the Hebrew people are said to have descended, specifically his great grandson *Heber*, whence derives *Hebrew* etymologically. Having begun to list Shem's descendants, the narrative breaks abruptly for the brief Tower of Babel interlude that kicks off Gen. 11.

Genesis 11

Following the Tower of Babel vignette, we quickly sort through more genealogy until we get to Abram/Abraham, the original Patriarch.

[KJV 606] TSB 359: *Your Savings 247*

The brief Tower of Babel anecdote recounts how Noah's descendants have begun moving eastward into Babylon (Shinar), where they begin to found civilization.[11a] Since humankind speaks a common language at this point, they are able to progress rapidly, firing bricks as building materials and so on. They decide to build themselves a city with a tower that reaches to the heavens, rather than scattering over the face of the Earth. Unfortunately, their Creator wants them to populate all of Creation, so he is less than pleased when he comes down and sees the tower.

Addressing the same divine companions to whom He spoke during the making of Man, he now shares his concerns about mankind's over-reaching.[11b] In order to thwart human plans, He and his Elohim helpers "go down" and confuse mankind's languages, reducing their ability to coordinate the massive building project. The humans give up on the city and tower as God disperses them.[11c]

The location of the partially finished tower is retroactively named Babel because there God confused the language of Man. One of the benefits of being an early member of mankind is that most places hadn't been named yet, so the naming rights were there for the taking.[11d]

With the unfortunate Babel incident behind us, we resume a genealogy of Shem's descendants, recounting nine more generations until we get Abram, who will become the key Patriarch of the Hebrew people.[11e] The narrative embraces the life and times of Abram/Abraham for the next fourteen chapters. Other key characters mentioned in the generational listings are Abram's father Terah[11f] and his nephew Lot. Both will figure in future events.

Abram marries Sarai (who will become "Sarah" after some adventures with Egypt's Pharaoh and God), who is beautiful but infertile. Terah takes Abram, Sarai and Lot, and they leave the Chaldean city of Ur (see map page 4) planning on going to Canaan.[11g] Remember this land would have been settled by Ham's son Canaan and his descendants nine generations and about five hundred years previously. But for whatever reason, the Abram clan doesn't make it to Canaan just yet, settling instead in Haran.[11h]

GENESIS 11 NOTES:

11a. In the Tower of Babel interlude, we see a reprise of key Genesis themes. Archeologists have unearthed similar tales in the writings of other civilizations such as Ugarit (Syria) and Sumerian (Iraq). The Ziggurat of Ur - still standing - is thought to be associated with the legend.

11b. God is never tempted to blame himself as Creator for a botched job, even though "they" are made in "our" image.

11c. God's territorial concern here is interesting, as his comments to his helpers/himself (Elohim) suggest he is worried once again (see Gen 2) about competition from mankind. This puts a spin on the insecurities of the early Hebrew deity seldom explored in Synagogue or Cathedral.

11d. The word Babel is interesting and may be related to the word babble and also to Babylon.

11e. We have already noted that Shem's grandson Heber lends his name to the Hebrew people. It is far from clear why it is he who gives his name to the Jewish people and not Abram/Abraham, as we never anything further about Heber.

11f. While Terah and his family are portrayed as idol *worshippers* in Genesis, there are extensive extra-biblical Jewish writings based on the tradition that Abram's father was a professional idol *manufacturer*. Additional medieval mystical Jewish stories revolve around Abram's enlightenment and its aftermath.

11g. Modern day Tall al Muqayyar, indicating the Patriarch of the Jewish nation was of Eastern Mesopotamian origin. He was born and raised in Ur, several hundred Km east of Canaan, not far from the Persian Gulf (present day eastern Iraq). As we look ahead, note that there are no "Israelites" in our story until Jacob's name is changed to Israel in Gen. 32. The Islamic tradition for the birthplace of Abraham is a different location.

11h. In present day Haran, about 600 Km northwest of Ur (see map page 4).

GENESIS 12 NOTES:

Date: ~ 1925 B.C

12a. Shechem is about 45 Km north of Jerusalem.

12b. *"And the Canaanite was then in the land."* [KJV]

12c. In Hebrew, "Beth" is house and "El" is God. Beth-el = House of God.

12d. Abram has told a cowardly lie and is willing to accept the Pharaoh's largess in return for the use of his wife. Pharaoh is not aware of the deception. In the context of the moral sense that the Bible is said to impart to its readers and students, it is unclear what crime Pharaoh has committed or why God views Abram as an upright individual.

Genesis 12

Abraham lends his wife to Pharaoh and comes out ahead in the deal.
First iteration of the Covenant.

[KJV 536] TSB 438: *Your Savings 98*

Although most people are familiar with the Lord's loathing of Pharaoh as found in the Exodus story (another 700+ years in the future), God first messes with the King of Egypt in Gen. 12. As is the case with many stories of this era, it is never clear what Pharaoh has done to draw God's ire.

As our story continues, God tells Abram to leave his new native country (Haran in present day Syria) and make his way to Canaan, along with Sarai, Lot and the rest of the clan. God indicates for the first but not the last time that he is going to make Abram's family a great nation; it is at this point that he could be said to have officially chosen the Chosen People. Abram's reaction to this news is not recorded as he travels to the great oak tree of Moreah at Shechem in Canaan.[12a]

Although the land of Canaan is currently occupied by Canaanites, God tells Abram that he is giving the land to him and his offspring, launching a conflict that will simmer for the next four thousand years.[12b] Abram builds an altar to the Lord, then heads for the hills east of Bethel, where he builds another altar.[12c] Then he heads for the Negev, the desert that separates Palestine from Egypt. Because there is a severe famine, the seventy-five year old Abram continues on to Egypt. This is the first of the Abramic family's trips down to Egypt, most of which turn out badly for the Egyptians.

Entering Egypt, Abram becomes paranoid about the beauty of his wife, fearing the Egyptians will kill him to get to his Sarai. So they tell the Egyptians Sarai is his sister. Sure enough, when Pharaoh's officials see Sarai, they take her to the palace to show the boss. This works out well for Abram, as he is given sheep, cattle, donkeys, servants and camels in payment for his "sister". We don't know how well it worked out for Sarai, but Pharaoh lets Abram know he has taken her as a wife. So Sarai is temporarily "married" to two men: one the Pharaoh, the other the Patriarch of the proto-Israelites.

All of this causes God to be angry with Pharaoh.[12d] He inflicts serious diseases on his household, the nature of which we are not told. Whatever the malady, Pharaoh makes the connection to Abram's sister, and summons him to share his feelings about the deception. The King of the Egyptians angrily sends Abram on his way, but allows him to keep Sarai and the other possessions he has acquired through Pharaoh's generosity.

Genesis 13

Abram and nephew Lot split up amicably. Lot moves to Sodom, with unfortunate consequences to come in a few chapters. God gives Canaan to Abram again.

[KJV 457] TSB 241: *Your Savings 216*

Abram has become very wealthy, not in small part because of Pharaoh's gifts. He returns with wife Sarai, nephew Lot, et al to the location of his first altar in Bethel. Unfortunately, both Lot and Abram have extensive livestock herds. Things get crowded and then tense, with fights breaking out among the herdsmen[13a]. The text notes again in passing that the original inhabitants - the Canaanites and Perizzites - were still there as well.

Abram tells his nephew, "Instead of fighting, let's split up. You pick the land you want and I'll go the other direction." Lot likes the looks of the Jordan river plain because it's well watered (a comparison is made to the Garden of Eden) and he heads southeast, settling near a party town called Sodom on the plains southeast of the Dead Sea.[13b]

Abram stays in Canaan. There is a foreshadowing of the problems to come, as a narrative interjection advises that this was before God destroyed Sodom, and that the men of Sodom are wicked.

After Lot departs, God gives Canaan to Abram again, inviting him to walk the length and breadth of the land.[13c] Abram moves his tents and goes to live near the great oak trees of Mamre[13d] near Hebron again, where he builds yet another altar to the Lord. Is it possible that God is so fond of Abram's altar building prowess that he is willing to overlook his recent moral lapse in Egypt?

GENESIS 13 NOTES:

13a. It is possible to envision pastoral martial arts scenes featuring shepherds wielding their staves with deadly force.

13b. Bad decision

13c. Second time God gives Canaan to Abram.

13d. Abraham will eventually acquire this land for a burial plot. In spite of God's repeated promises, it is the only land he will ever own. Shrines in tree groves were also associated early Canaanite cults for local deities.

GENESIS 14 NOTES:

14a. Ancient Elam was located in southwest Iran, east of Mesopotamia and well northeast of Sodom. "Elam" was also another son of Shem. Extra-biblical sources describe a Chededorlaomer as a major King/warlord, but of a much later era.

14b. This brief episode is the only event involving Melchizedek in Genesis. Even so, the identity of Melchizedek has been disputed for thousands of years. Gen. 14 is certainly the first mention of a *priest* of any kind in the Bible, but the official Aaronite priesthood won't be established until hundreds of years in the future. We are left to speculate as to whom this individual is supposed to be. Some traditions identify him as Noah's son Shem, others as Philitis, builder of the great Pyramid of Egypt. It has also been variously conjectured that he is an Elohim (one of God's helpers) or a member of an alien race that bred with humans to create the Nephilim or a magician or Jesus practicing for later. He is mentioned twice more in Bible but remains a mystery. In an anthropological context, Melchizedek was most likely a shaman, as the roles of priests, magicians, shamans and dream interpreters were indistinguishable during the Bronze age.

14c. Ancient Hebrew had no vowels, so S-L-M is thought to refer to either "peace" (Salam or Shalom in modern Arabic and Hebrew) or Shalim, the god of dusk in the Canaanite religion

14d. We will note in passing that Pharaoh had already done that in payment for the use of his wife Sarai.

Genesis 14

With his 318 man army and some divine luck, Abram rescues his nephew Lot from Chedorlaomer, King of Elam. We also meet the enigmatic Melchizedek for the first time.

[KJV 606] TSB 316: *Your Savings 290*

Next thing you know, there is a nine king war in the Vale of Siddim, the region southeast of the Dead Sea. On one side are four kings from Mesopotamia: the kingpin Chedorlaomer of Elam and three vassal kings who support him.[14a] This group battles five insurgent kings of the southern plains. The rebel region includes Sodom and Gomorrah near where Lot and his people have settled. The Chedorlaomer faction wins the battle, loots Sodom and Gomorrah, captures Lot's family and heads north with their booty.

A battle survivor makes his way to Hebron and tells Abram of his nephew's plight. Abram assembles 318 trained men and goes after Chedorlaomer and his king buddies. At Dan, Abram divides up his warriors and attacks the enemy camp at night. Not only does his tiny force rout the four armies, but they pursue them all the way to Damascus (about 200 km) and beyond. Abram recovers his nephew and the stolen possessions and brings everyone back home. These are three hundred eighteen tough hombres.

The key event of this chapter is when an individual named *Melchizedek* comes out to meet Abram, bringing bread and wine.[14b] Melchizedek is the King of Salem (which is Jerusalem[14c]) and also a priest of God the Most High. He blesses Abram and also the Creator, to whom he attributes Abram's unlikely victory. Abram gives him one tenth of the spoils of war.

The King of Sodom is now in a mood to deal and suggests Abram give him back the kidnapped population and keep the spoils for himself. Abram, suddenly adverse to receiving gifts, refuses to take anything from the King of Sodom (not even the thread of a sandal). According to his statement, he doesn't want anyone to be able to say the King of Sodom made him rich.[14d] He therefore accepts only what his men have eaten and sees to it they get their share of the spoils.

Genesis 15

This is a perplexing, slightly hallucinogenic, good-news bad-news chapter in which God gives Abram mixed messages about the future. The Lord also reviews the Covenant for the third and fourth times.

[KJV 471] TSB 408: *Your Savings 63*

The chapter starts with a "vision of God's voice", in which the Lord is reassuring Abram that he has his back. But, in a behavior pattern that will repeat itself throughout the Old Testament, Abram complains that he has no children, and that his legal heir at this point is Eliezer of Damascus, his servant and head of household. God reassures Abram that he will have a natural son, and repeats the promise regarding voluminous progeny. Abram takes him at His word. God also repeats the promise regarding the gift of land[15a], which Abram also accepts, but with the caveat that he is now looking for a little clarification on the timeline.[15b]

By way of answer, God requests a sacrifice consisting of a heifer, a goat and a ram, each three years old, along with a dove and a young pigeon.[15c] Abram assembles these animals and sacrifices them by cutting them in half except for the birds.

As the sun sets and with the animal parts still sitting there, Adam falls into a "thick and dreadful" sleep. Although it can be read differently, this "horror of great darkness" seems to fall upon him while he is already in the middle of a vision. It is a dream within a vision, if you will, so his spiritual state is quite complex. At this point, God radically changes his tone and tells Abram some bad news about the future.

Having just confirmed the covenant for the third time, God now reveals that Abram's descendants will be strangers in a strange land, enslaved and mistreated for four hundred years. To allay Abram's misgivings, God promises that he will punish the nation that enslaves them and that his descendants will emerge with additional wealth.[15d]

Having shared this prophecy, God assures Abram that he himself will live long and prosper. Abram's people will return to this land after four generations, the reason for the delay being that the Amorites currently living there have not yet reached a level of wickedness that warrants their destruction.

At this point, the sun has set, and a smoking firepot and torch pass among the animal parts laid out for the sacrifice. Having done this, God repeats his covenant again, this time specifying the exact borders of the promised territory: *"from the river of Egypt to the great river, the Euphrates"* [KJV]. The land contract has expanded to include the land of the Kenites, Kenizzites, Kadmonites, Hittites, Perizzites, Rephaites, Amorites, Canaanites, Girgashites and Jebusites. [15e]

GENESIS 15 NOTES:

15a. This is the third time God promises the land to Abraham, along with descendants that "will number as the stars".

15b. He is already living peacefully and prosperously in the land God has promised, so the issue would appear to be the actual deed of ownership. Abram seems to have relatively harmonious relationships with the locals. The real problems arise when the Israelites attempt to actually exercise their ownership option several centuries in the future.

15c. Again, the elevated importance of animal sacrifice in a context difficult for modern readers to understand. Note, however, the accent on very specific sacrifices many centuries prior to God spelling out sacrificial responsibilities and rituals in Exodus and Leviticus.

15d. Clearly a foreshadowing of the Joseph - Moses saga to come.

15e. This is the fourth time God has announced the Covenant and the gift of land. In the process, the promised Israel-estate tract has steadily expanded as new boundaries are laid out in Genesis. The property now includes Palestine, Syria, Iraq and part of Turkey and Egypt. This is a lot of territory - much greater than even the amorphous "Canaan". Neither the territory of King David's legendary second millennium B.C. kingdom nor that of the modern state of Israel has ever equaled this area. Nevertheless, this land survey is used by extreme elements in modern Israel to justify "Greater Israel", and to fire the imagination of American right wing Christians. This holy tract is envisioned as headquarters for the Millennium Kingdom, the 1,000-year reign of Jesus Christ, the Bridegroom of the Church and the King of the Jews. Talk about mission creep.

GENESIS 16 NOTES:

16a. David makes an almost identical statement to King Saul after he cuts off part of the king's fighting skirt (Samuel 24:12). Saul and David had a complicated relationship.

16b. So, it's a trade off. Yes, Hagar, you are going to have uncounted descendants, but your son is going to be pretty much of a violent lunatic who can't quite cope with civilized society. This prediction is setting up the upcoming revelation that Ishmael will be the father of the Arabic peoples. Ishmael is considered the ancestor of Mohammed.

16c. Beer-Lahai-Ro means "well of the Living One who sees me".

Genesis 16

The childless Sarai persuades Abram to sire a child with her maidservant Hagar, then wishes she hadn't. Hagar also wishes she hadn't as her son Ishmael's future is foretold by God.

[KJV 412] TSB 298: *Your Savings 114*

With all this behind us, we discover that Sarai is still childless after ten years living in Canaan. She suggests that Abram sleep with her Egyptian maidservant Hagar (probably acquired from the Pharaoh deal) to see if he can get anything going. Note that in the previous chapter, God doesn't specify whom the mother of Abram's heir will be, so this work around doesn't seem to violate any understandings Abram has with God. So Abram takes Hagar as an additional wife. No sooner does Abram impregnate Hagar than the uppity servant girl begins to 'dis' Sarai.

Sarai climbs all over Abram, blaming him for the situation even thought it was her idea. She says famously: *"The Lord judge between you and me."* [16a] With Abram's permission, Sarai mistreats Hagar and the servant runs away. At this point God needs to get involved, sending an angel (or messenger) to find Hagar near a spring. He advises her to get home and submit to her mistress. Echoing his boss's previous statements, the angel tells Hagar that her offspring will be multitudinous. He also lets her know that her impending child will be a son by the name of Ishmael, which, according to the messenger, connotes that God had heard of Hagar's misery. The rest of the news is not so good. This Ishmael is going to be a *"wild donkey of a man"*, who lives in the wilderness and fights with everyone around him. [16b] No Mom wants to hear that.

Hagar concludes from this conversation that she has seen God himself and lived, which was counter to the expectations at the time. The well is named Beer-Lahai-Roi. [16c]

As foretold, at the age of eighty-six, Abram finds himself father of Ishmael, son of his wife's Egyptian servant.

Genesis 17

God announces the covenant again and changes Abram and Sarai's names. All the guys get mandatory circumcisions.

[KJV 679] TSB 324: *Your Savings 355*

Thirteen years later, God gets back in touch with Abram and suggests they go for a walk; he casually commands Abram to be perfect. He confirms the covenant once more and again mentions the great numbers he envisions for Abram's descendants.[17a] Abram falls facedown, possibly because he has heard this quite a few times before, but God continues with the predictions.

Because he is going to be the father of many nations, God renames Abram *Abraham*.[17b] God continues on for a while with variations on the original covenant, remarking several times that he expects to be the God of Abraham's descendants as a condition of the land deal. He then off-handedly mentions Abraham's side of the covenant bargain, which is when we first hear the circumcision clause. All males are to be circumcised, with Abraham leading from the front.[17c] This requirement includes not only Abraham's direct descendants, but also any servants or slaves that might be purchased. God warns that anyone not circumcised will be "cut off" from his people, an ominous choice of words.

God also changes Sarai's name to Sarah, because she is going to be the mother of a major multitude. Although he has already fallen down, Abraham again falls down, this time chuckling behind God's back about the latest prophecy. He is ninety-nine and Sarah is ninety, so Abraham doubts they are likely to become parents at their age.[17d]

Abraham suggests that God must mean that Ishmael will be the one to enjoy all these blessings, and that would be just fine with him, but God says no, that's not the deal. Sarah will have a son and he will be named Isaac. The covenant will be with Isaac. For his part, Ishmael will be the father of twelve rulers, but will not get the covenant deal.

To conclude the chapter, God leaves and Abraham circumcises every male in his family and household. Ishmael, thirteen at the time, is included. [17e]

GENESIS 17 NOTES:

17a. This is the fifth proclamation of the great news about the covenant.

17b. Hebrew = Avraham

17c. One year shy of his hundredth birthday, this can't be good news for Abraham, who will supply the foreskin of his forefathers. It is also probable that domestic help around the region did their best to avoid being purchased by Abraham's clan.

17d. This reaction makes sense from a modern perspective, but is surprising coming from Abraham. His recent ancestors were just getting warmed up at 500 years of age or so. What has changed?

17e. A painful Bar Mitzva.

GENESIS 18 NOTES:

Date: ~ 1900 B.C.

18a. *"Three men stood over against him."* [KJV] The pluralistic nature of God / Elohim is once again manifested without explanation. There are explicitly three men visiting Abraham. Two of them make their way to check out Sodom while the singular "Lord" stays to chat with Abraham.

18b. The text has obliquely foreshadowed the destruction of Sodom and Gomorrah, but Abraham has not yet been told what's coming.

18c. Throughout the Pentateuch, God is very much hands on, to the point that he must be "on location" to acquire information. When the Christians appropriated the Hebrew's ancient deity, the personal God component went along. In the process, expectations regarding the new God's ability to directly affect individual lives remained high, perhaps unrealistically so.

18d. That's right.

18e. Throughout the Old Testament, God is rarely concerned with collateral damage, so this is an exception.

18f. But as we will soon see, even ten righteous people is more than Sodom can come up with. Sodom and Gomorrah are generally mentioned together as "towns to avoid" on the plains of Shinar, but Sodom seems to be in a league of its own. You can't be arrested in Georgia for any activity derived from the word "Gomorrah".

Genesis 18

Sarah gets in trouble for doubting God and his angel friends; the Sodomites are about to be investigated for excessive partying.

[KJV 867] TSB 475: *Your Savings 392*

In the heat of the day, Abraham is sitting in the doorway of his tent when three men appear on the plains. This situation is described as the *Lord* appearing to him, and we note that Abraham also addresses the three men collectively as "my Lord."[18a]

He begs the men to stop by, rest, eat, and get their feet washed. He instructs Sarah to start baking some bread. As for Abraham, he goes and selects a choice, tender calf, some curds and so on, and serves his guests. The men ask where Sarah is, and Abraham tells them she is in the tent. Then, the Lord in the singular tells him that he/they will return in a year, and Sarah will be the mother of a son at that point.

Sarah is listening, and the narrator reminds us again that both she and Abraham are well advanced in years, which, once again, is odd when we consider the life spans his recent ancestors have enjoyed. Sarah laughs in her tent, scoffing at the idea that motherhood is in her future. Either God hears her or He is omniscient, but He asks Abraham why she doubts Him. God and Sarah have a brief argument as to whether or not she laughed, but the Lord gets the last Word.

This spat seems to blow over, and Abraham walks the composite Lord to the door of the tent. Here, they look over in the direction of Sodom, and the Lord wonders aloud to his angelic companions - or to Himself - whether He should tell Abraham about His plans, which seem to be related to Sodom. Considering that Abraham is going to head up a mighty nation that will follow His ways (muses the Lord), the Lord concludes that Abraham should probably be in the picture.[18b]

Standing outside Abraham's tent, the Lord tells him there have been so many complaints about the sinfulness of Sodom and Gomorrah that He as God feels compelled to check out the stories personally.[18c] So the two other men who are part of the three-way deity depart for Sodom, leaving Abraham standing before the Lord[18d].

Although the text doesn't specifically mention it, attentive readers will recall that Abraham's nephew Lot is living among the Sodomites. This accounts for Abraham's anxious temerity in addressing God outside his tent. He asks God if He would sweep away the righteous with the wicked.[18e] He even lectures God a bit, asking if "the Judge of all the Earth won't do the right thing?" God agrees to spare the city if there are fifty righteous people in the city.

Abraham presses his luck, and manages through a painful progression of passive-aggressive queries to reduce the minimum number of righteous people required to avoid destruction. He gets God down to ten.[18f]

The Lord departs and Abraham goes back into his tent.

Genesis 19

The Sodomites want to party with the angelic visitors, but Lot offers them his daughters instead. Later, after his wife is a pillar of salt, Lot's daughters have their way with Dad as he becomes the father of two more Middle Eastern peoples.

[KJV 1108] TSB 537: *Your Savings 571*

Meanwhile, the same two angels arrive at the city gates of Sodom in the evening, and as luck would have it, none other than Abraham's nephew Lot is there to greet them. Lot bows and implores them to spend the night at his house, but they initially turn him down. He is adamant, and they end up enjoying an excellent meal at this house. Meanwhile, the citizens of Sodom have their own thoughts on hospitality. They surround the house and demand that Lot send the men (angels) out for a homosexual rape fiesta. [19a]

Lot goes outside and tries to talk them out of it. He offers instead his two virgin daughters and tells the Sodom party crowd they can "do what they like with them."[19b]

All he manages to do is aggravate the Sodomites even more, and they begin to threaten him. Comments are made suggesting Lot is an undocumented alien in Sodom, one who now presumes to judge his hosts. Luckily the angels are able to pull him back inside and close the door. They also take the precaution of striking the Sodomites blind.

The men[19c] apparently have seen enough of the people of Sodom and inform Lot that he should gather his sons, daughters and fiancées and prepare to leave Sodom. They have been sent to destroy the place.[19d] His daughters' fiancées think Lot is joking, so they lose their opportunity to continue living.

At dawn, the angels tell Lot to take his wife and daughters and get the hell out of town. Lot, who seems to be a bit of a professional victim, hesitates, and the angels have to lead him to safety. He is told to flee to the mountains and not look back.

Lot complicates matters a bit by insisting they escape to the small town of Zoar instead; in spite of him, things get rolling as the sun is rising in the sky. The angels rain burning sulfur down on Sodom and Gomorrah, as well as the other cities of the sinful plain. He/they wipe out all the people and vegetation.

Lot's wife looks back and she is turned into a pillar of salt.[19e]

Abraham arises the next morning to see smoke coming from the devastated plains, as Lot and his two daughters leave Zoar and settle in a cave in the mountains. At some point, his daughters grow weary of living in the cave, and also realize that with their former fiancées now fried, there is a serious shortage of men. Plus, Mom is a pillar of salt, so Dad is probably a little lonely. The elder of the two suggests to her sister that they get Lot drunk on wine and have sex with him while he is inebriated.[19f]

On successive nights, the daughters ply Lot with wine and get to know him in the Biblical sense. [19g] Both of them become pregnant as a result. The older daughter has a son named Moab, who becomes the father of the Moabites. The younger bears a son named Ben-Ammi who is the forebear of the Ammonites. It will be more than five centuries before the Israelites escaping Egypt will come into prolonged conflict with both of these peoples, who have also settled in the interim in the Promised Land. [19h]

GENESIS 19 NOTES:

19a. To be clear, every single version of the Bible that could be considered mainstream says exactly the same thing: *send them out so we can have sex with them*. Hence the term "Sodomize".

A virtually identical story about locals wanting to party with visitors is recounted in Judges 19 -21.

19b. We discover shortly that both these daughters are engaged to be married. Lot is clearly obsessive about the requirements of hospitality, as he would rather give up his daughters for a gang rape than have anything happen to those under the protection of his roof.

19c. Who are simultaneously angels and agents of God.

19d. The last time God was this aggravated it rained for forty days and nights, but this time it rains fire.

19e. This event echoes similar regional myths explaining the origins of salt deposits in the area. Generally, the affected individual turns into a pillar after seeing a god.

19f. This coupling establishes another Old Testament pattern: women who commit incest with family members in order to become pregnant. In this case, the stated objective is to preserve the family line.

19g. It isn't clear how this is managed. If he is drunk enough to not notice this is his daughter, then his ability to perform the deed could indeed be classified as another Bible miracle.

19h. The narrative has now discredited the ancestry of the Canaanites, the Arabs, the Moabites and the Ammonites.

GENESIS 20 NOTES:

20a. We are aware from previous chapters that Sarah is ninety and considers herself advanced in years. Nevertheless, she is apparently still babe-ular enough to incite the lust of the local Philistine King Abimelech.

Without giving away the whole story, we will note that claiming one's wife to be one's sister will turn out to be an Abrahamic family trait in Gen. 26.

The accuracy of both this story and the previous Pharaohic misunderstanding is questioned by Islamic scholars, primarily because by Islamic definition, the Patriarch Abraham could not have been such a schmuck. These scholars accuse the Jews of making up these stories. God forbid.

20b. Southeast of present day Gaza and west of the Dead Sea (see map, page 4).

20c. A half truth, as it turns out.

20d. In these scenarios, God never reveals why he didn't prevent Abraham from lying to Abimelech, thus saving everyone a lot of trouble.

20e. This seems disingenuous from the man who defeated mighty King Chedorlaomer and three other king's armies with only 318 men.

20f. This is the first we are hearing of this relationship, but nevertheless, half-sister is quite a different concept than sister in terms of biological implications. She is still his wife. So much for Honest Abe.

20g. Suggesting that Sarah had been a concubine in waiting for more than just a few days.

Genesis 20

Abraham reprises the "sister" act with King Abimelech[20a], with better results for the King and plenty more luxury goods for Abraham.

[KJV 498] TSB 353: *Your Savings 145*

The ever restless Abraham moves south to Gerar, which is in the kingdom of Abimelech.[20b] Not one to reinvent the wheel, Abraham once again represents Sarah as his sister.[20c] The King quickly appropriates her as a potential wife, but doesn't have time to consummate the relationship. Nevertheless, God is angry at Abimelech and threatens his life in a dream.

One has to appreciate the King James Version of this conversation: *"But God came to Abimelech in a dream by night, and said to him, Behold, thou art but a dead man, for the woman which thou hast taken; for she is a man's wife."* [KJV]

Abimelech proves feistier than the Pharaoh, pointing out accurately that not only had Abraham lied to him, but he himself hasn't touched the elderly chick in any case. God now acknowledges that the King has a point, but reveals the reason Abimelech didn't get it on with Sarah is because God Himself benevolently prevented it for Abimelech's own good.[20d] So all he has to do is return Sarah and God is willing to overlook the crime Abimelech didn't know he was committing.

To make sure God drops the charges, Abimelech once again lays some serious largess on Abraham, not the least of which is 1,000 shekels of silver and some female slaves. No harm, no foul. But he does take the opportunity to complain to Abraham again about the lie.

The Patriarch replies once again that he was afraid that he would be killed for his wife.[20e] He now reveals for the first time that he wasn't exactly lying, because Sarah is his half-sister.[20f] He has asked Sarah to describe Abraham as her brother as a way of showing her love.

In order to set things right, Abraham prays to God and lets him know that Sarah has been returned with interest. God gets the news and returns the females of Abimelech's household to their former levels of fertility. As it turns out, and as we are discovering for the first time, God had closed the wombs of every woman in the King's household.[20g] Ouch.

Genesis 21

Water wells are a common theme connecting the two sections of this chapter, as Isaac is finally born, Hagar gets thrown out into the desert and Abraham and Abimelech seal a water treaty with sheep.

[KJV 774] TSB 475: *Your Savings 299*

As promised, Sarah becomes pregnant and gives birth to Isaac, who is immediately circumcised by his Dad. Sarah's first impression is that everyone will enjoy her good fortune, saying, "everyone who hears this will laugh with me."

She's almost right, the exception being Ishmael[21a], who mocks her newborn son Isaac at his weaning ceremony. Ever the diva, Sarah demands that Abraham throw Hagar and her son out of the household so that Isaac doesn't have to share the inheritance.[21b] At first this troubles Abraham, but God tells him not to worry because he is going to make Ishmael into a mighty nation as well.[21c] This apparently mollifies Abraham as he sends Hagar and Ishmael out into the desert (the modern Negev), making sure to provide some food and a skin of water. The text describes Hagar setting Ishmael on her shoulders as she heads out the door into the desert . This was above and beyond the call of duty and might have raised some eyebrows, as Ishmael would have been about fourteen years old by this time.

Hagar wanders in the desert for a while. When the water runs out, she places the teenage boy under a bush and moves away out of sight, commenting that she doesn't want to watch him die. Luckily, an angel has been assigned to Hagar, instructing her to lift the boy up and take him by the hand. God then opens her eyes and she is now able to see a water well she had somehow overlooked. She fills the skin with water again and gives the boy a drink.[21d]

We are given a glimpse of the future, learning that God will be with Ishmael as he grows up in the Desert of Paran. He will become proficient at archery and his mom will quite understandably find a nice Egyptian girl to be his wife.[21e]

About the time Hagar is trying to find water for her son, Abimelech opens a new dialog with Abraham, asking him to promise never to deal falsely with him or his descendants. Based on Abimelech's previous experience with Abraham, this is a savvy move. Abraham swears the oath as requested, but unfortunately there is an immediate dispute over a well that had been seized by Abimelech's servants. To resolve it, Abraham gives some cattle and sheep to Abimelech as a means of sealing the treaty, with an additional seven ewes set aside as witness that the well was dug by Abraham.[21f]

The two members of this desert nobility name the place where the oath was sworn *Beersheba* (the Well of the Oath or Seven Wells). Abraham also plants a tamarisk tree, which enables him to call upon the name of the Lord.[21g]

After the treaty has been made at Beersheba, Abimelech returns to the land of the Philistines. Abraham also stays in the land of the Philistines for a long time.[21h]

GENESIS 21 NOTES:

21a. Son of her Egyptian slave Hagar.

21b. You'd think that after having been the wife of a Pharaoh, the pre-concubine of a local King and the on and off wife of the Patriarch of the Chosen People, Sarah would lighten up a little.

21c. But not as mighty as Isaac's nation.

21d. Ishmael is not named in this chapter.

21e. This vignette would account for God's prediction back in Gen. 16 that Ishmael is going to be something of a wild man living in the wilderness. If he does develop a chip on his shoulder, it might be attributable to having been thrown out into the desert by his Dad.

21f. A modern reader might well be tempted to wonder about Abraham's moral imperatives, having sent his concubine and son out into the Negev desert, while negotiating with the local chieftain over water rights. In this particular instance, Christian apologists almost unanimously point out that his transgression is excused because he was operating on the instructions of God's angel, and God fully intended to find a well for Hagar.

21g. To a nomadic people, the planting of a tamarisk tree would symbolize that Abraham expects his descendants to remain in the area for many generations. Throughout this section of Genesis, we should be aware that in spite of his wealth, Abraham is a dweller in tents. As nomads, his people are only able to inhabit lands at the pleasure of the more urbanized civilizations around them.

21h. The abrupt Philistine reference is explained partially by the fact that national boundaries were not fixed during the Bronze Age. Described as Ham's descendants, most archeologists associate them with Aegean or proto-Greek "Sea Peoples" culture. However, the time of Abraham is several hundred years before the Philistines were in this area, according to archeological evidence.

GENESIS 22 NOTES:

22a. Since Abraham is prepared to murder and burn his son, there is no particular reason at this point to over think telling Isaac a little white lie.

22b. Isaac's reaction is not recorded, however, we can well imagine his relief when the angel interrupts the sacrifice and calls the whole thing off. Does he high-five his Dad for passing God's test? We can't know for certain, but we can speculate that had this event taken place in the twenty-first century, Isaac would have been in therapy the rest of his life.

22c. The clear moral context in the early days of the OT God Elohim/JHWH - who will morph into the Christian God - is that obedience to Him trumps any other consideration.

22d. Or Jehovah-Jerah. A lesser man than the Patriarch would have named it "the place where I almost killed my son and burnt him on the altar."

22e. Sixth celebration of the covenant by God via his angel, who vacillates between speaking on God's behalf, speaking as God, and referring to God in the third person, a further manifestation of the plural and ambiguous identity of Elohim-JHWH.

Genesis 22

God tests Abraham by ordering him to sacrifice his son Isaac as a burnt offering; later, Abraham's brother Nahor has twelve children.

[KJV 629] TSB 253: *Your Savings 376*

God's obsession with sacrifices reaches a new and unsettling level as he tells Abraham to sacrifice his son Isaac. To add insult to injury, he sends him three days journey away to a mountain near Moriah to off his kid. No reason is given either for the sacrifice or the distant location.

Abraham sets off with his servants, whom he leaves behind once the destination is reached. He proceeds to the site, making Isaac carry the firewood while he carries the knife and fire. The boy notices that the sacrificial lamb is missing and inquires about the oversight. Abraham lies to his son[22a], telling him "God will provide the sacrifice."

Nevertheless, Isaac may well have felt some anxiety as Abraham built the altar, tied him to it and raised the knife.[22b] Luckily, just at that moment, the angel calls out to Abraham and tells him to leave Isaac alone. He is satisfied now that Abraham has presented sufficient evidence that he fears God, which was the ultimate objective of the exercise.[22c]

Abraham discovers a ram caught in the thicket and sacrifices it instead, calling the place Jahweh-Jireh. This means "the Lord will provide".[22d] He returns to Beersheba.

God takes this dramatic opportunity to reiterate the basic covenant promises for the sixth time, in much the same language as used previously.[22e]

Somewhat anticlimactically, Abraham is told about the eight children born to his brother Nahor via his regular wife Milcah, and four more kids courtesy of his concubine. We will meet up with Nahor's offspring soon.

Genesis 23

Sarah dies and Abraham makes a deal with the Hittites for a burial site.

[KJV 539] TSB 194: *Your Savings 345*

Due to a number of longwinded conversations in the original, this chapter allows *True Scripture* to save you a lot of time. In Gen. 23, Sarah dies in the Canaanite town of Hebron at the age of a hundred and twenty seven.[23a] Journeying to Hebron (presumably from the Gerar/Beersheba desert to the south), Abraham weeps for his wife.[23b] After mourning, he approaches the local Hittites about purchasing a burial site for Sarah, pointing out that he is but an alien and sojourner in their land.[23c]

These particular Hittites are nothing if not accommodating and after some discussion, Abraham purchases the Cave of Machpelah from Ephron son of Zohar for four hundred shekels. Judging from their conversation with Abraham, Ephron and his friends seem to be stand up guys, especially considering they are descendants of Ham.

GENESIS 23 NOTES:

23a. Hebron, or Kiriath Arba is located about 31 km south of Jerusalem within the present boundaries of the West Bank. This city is an important site throughout the Old Testament and is considered by Jewish writers to be the burial site of the three Patriarchs. The seemingly minor event described in Gen. 23 is a prelude to a lot of future burials of key proto-Israelites. What this story would not reveal to a modern reader is this location is Judaism's second most holy site after the Temple of the Mount. Islam and Christianity also regard the site as sacred.

The *Oaks of Mamre* which attracted Abraham in his youth are located here as well. Back in the midsts of archeological antiquity, the site was a Canaanite shrine dedicated to the supreme sky god El. He was the most powerful of the Canaanite divine pantheon.

23b. Whether or not her ex husband Pharaoh or King Abimelech made it to the funeral is unrecorded.

23c These are the "biblical Hittites" said to be descended from Canaan's son Heth. They are traditionally considered one of the twelve Canaanite nations. However, they are not the same as the historical Hittite Empire, which dominated Anatolia (Turkey) much later in history. For our purpoises, "Hittites" are the same as "Canaanites".

GENESIS 24 NOTES:

24a. Although unnamed, the servant is probably Eliezer of Damascus, as referenced in Gen. 15.

24b. If Sarah has died at the age of 127, then Isaac is now in his late thirties.

24c. It is worth repeating that Abraham is technically not a Jew at this point, but is rather of Mesopotamian/Iraqi stock. As a direct descendant of Shem's great grandson Heber, he qualifies as a "Hebrew", but there will be no Israelites for two more generations, and no Jews until the formation of a "nation" from the tribe of Judah.

24d. A town a few Km south of Haran and probably named for Abraham's brother.

24e. The very much interactive God of Genesis is willing at this point to take suggestions regarding such procedures. Compare and contrast with later versions of the deity as he evolves into the Christian God.

24f. She is also Isaac's cousin. We see now that the news of Nahor's successful breeding initiative was tacked onto the end of Gen. 22 for a reason.

24g. Laban's relationship with his nephew Jacob will reveal him to be of a deviously materialistic nature.

Genesis 24

Abraham sends a servant[24a] off to find a wife for Isaac; with the help of God, the servant finds Rebekah at a well and brings her back.

[KJV 1816] TSB 687: *Your Savings 1129*

The chapter begins with Abraham telling his chief servant to put his hand under his thigh, but it turns out it's only for the purpose of swearing an oath. Abraham wants the servant to promise he will go find his son Isaac a wife, but not among the Canaanites where they are living now.[24b] He insists the servant go back to Ur whence Abraham originally came and find a wife there among his people;[24c] if the woman doesn't want to come back to marry Isaac, the servant will be released from his oath. However, he is adamant that the servant not take Isaac back to Ur. Abraham mentions God's promise to give him Canaan, and as it turns out, the deity has also offered (in a previously unrecorded conversation) to send an angel to help out with the wife-finding mission.

The servant accepts the assignment by placing his hand under Abraham's thigh, then heads for Mesopotamia with ten camels and all kinds of excellent gifts to help any potential bride-to-be make the right decision. Arriving at the town of Nahor, he heads immediately for the well, knowing the women will be coming around to draw water.[24d] Here he prays to God for success in his mission. He even suggests a scenario for success: that the girl he asks for a drink of water will also offer to water his camels.[24e]

By way of immediate answer, who should be arriving at the well just then but the lovely Rebekah, granddaughter of Abraham's brother Nahor.[24f] This is the kind of coincidence only God can arrange, considering the short turnaround. Not only is Rebekah beautiful and accommodating, she is also a virgin. He asks her for a drink and sure enough, she also offers to draw water for his camels, which she does with enthusiasm. This is clearly primo wife material, so the servant pulls out a gold nose ring weighing a beka and two gold arm bracelets weighing ten shekels apiece. Bestowing these gifts on her, he inquires as to her lineage and asks for accommodations for the night. Rebekah tells him there is plenty of straw, fodder and room, and the servant praises the Lord for making his trip a success.

When Rebekah returns home and shows her brother Laban the nose ring and arm bracelets, he naturally heads back to the well to meet the man with the gifts.[24g] Noting that the servant has obviously been blessed by the Lord, he insists he and his camels come back to the house immediately.

Genesis 24 continued

Before dining, the servant tells Laban he wants to state his mission. This he does in scrupulous detail, rehashing the narrative in virtually the same words we've already read. When he has made his case for Rebekah to come back to Canaan as Isaac's bride-to-be, Laban indicates that the whole encounter is clearly the work of the Lord and that Rebekah should by all means do as God has directed.[24h] The servant is so pleased that he pulls out even more goodies: gold, silver and nice clothes for Rebekah and unspecified costly gifts for Laban and Bethuel. The evening ends with a party.

However, as the servant prepares to leave the next morning, Laban and his Mom ask if Rebekah can stay behind for another ten days. The servant objects, so they leave it to Rebekah, who decides to leave immediately. She, along with her nurse, leave for Canaan after receiving her brother's blessings.

Meanwhile, Isaac has been living in the Negev desert further south, presumably engaged in livestock management on behalf of Abraham.[24i] One day, returning from Beer Lahai Roi he goes out for his evening meditation and sees camels approaching.[24j] Rebekah inquires who it is coming to meet them, and is told by the stalwart servant that it is indeed his master's son and her betrothed. Rebekah accordingly covers herself with a veil.

Once the servant has explained the whole story, Isaac takes Rebekah "into the tent of his mother" and "marries" her.[24k] Isaac's love for Rebekah comforts him after his Mother's death.

GENESIS 24 NOTES (continued):

24h. In this era, it was not unusual for powerful tribal leaders to associate themselves with specific gods or have personal cults. Abraham left his father's family and now identifies himself with Elohim. But Laban and his family remain idolaters, so Laban's comment about the Lord suggests although he considers Abraham's personal god to be unusually powerful, he also considers Him one of many.

24i. Possibly explaining his lack of interest thus far in finding his own bride.

24j. (Also Kadesh-barnea) This is the same well where God told Hagar of his plans for Ishmael back in Gen. 16.

24k. The exact nature of the marriage ceremony is not described.

GENESIS 25 NOTES:

Date: ~ 1825 BC.

25a. At the beginning of Gen. 25, we know that Abraham is older than 137 years but younger than 175 years (his official life span). In the interim between Sarah's death and his own, he has the time and the wherewithal to impregnate Keturah at least six times (six times with sons, as the birth of daughters is not reported).

25b. Midianites will play an ambiguous role in the Joseph sequence that ends the Book of Genesis.

25c. It is interesting that the "wild man" Ishmael returns from somewhere out in the desert to bury his father.

25d. The Qur'an contradicts the Hebrew writings on many points of Ishmael's lineage. Note, however, the Islamic writings could not have been compiled until at least 1000 years after the Torah was written down and 2,500 years after the Abrahamic era.

Later in Genesis, it will be Ishmaelites that purchase handsome Joseph from his brothers and sell him to Potiphar, thus initiating a sub plot that ends 400 years later in Exodus.

25e. Isaac is said to be forty when he marries Rebekah and sixty when the twins are born. Abraham would be one-hundred sixty when the twins were born. Thus, the Esau and Jacob story does not follow this part of the Ishmael narrative chronologically, but takes us back in time. Assuming Rebekah to be a minimum of fourteen when she marries Isaac, she would be at least thirty-four when the twins are born.

Genesis 25

Abraham takes on another wife and fathers several more nations. Later, Jacob serves his twin brother Esau a very expensive meal.

[KJV 697] TSB 513: *Your Savings 184*

Unlike many widowers well over a hundred years old, Abraham picks up the pieces after Sarah's death and marries Keturah.[25a] As listed in this chapter, Abraham's newest set of descendants account for the origins of the Midianites and several other biblical peoples and place names.[25b] Over the years, Abraham has apparently also had a number of unnamed concubines as well. Although Isaac is to be his only official heir, the Patriarch does give gifts to the sons of his concubines before sending them away to the East.

Abraham dies at a hundred and seventy-five and is buried by Isaac and Ishmael in the same cave near Hebron he had previously purchased from Ephron the Hittite in Gen. 23.[25c] Isaac goes back to live near the Beer Lahai Roi well in the desert.

Ishmael's twelve sons are now recorded for posterity. They are described as twelve tribal rulers, the same way that Jacob's sons will be characterized in future chapters. Ishmael then dies at the age of one hundred thirty seven. The tribes that comprise his offspring settle to the east of Egypt in an area described as "Havilah to Shur". Once again, the narrative is at pains to discredit Ishmael's descendants, depicting them as existing in a state of hostility with surrounding peoples (who are also their relatives).[25d]

The story picks up again with the famous but bizarre saga of the dueling twins, Esau and Jacob. Isaac is forty when he marries Rebekah, and the infertility problem that plagued his mom Sarah crops up again. This time, a prayer to the Lord solves the problem, but the process that is described in one sentence in the text requires about nineteen years to incubate.[25e]

Once Rebekah has become pregnant, the two fetuses jostle each other to the point that she feels compelled to ask God what's going on. God explains that two nations are in her womb: one people will be stronger than the other and the older brother will serve the younger. The two nations emerge as twin brothers Esau and Jacob, the latter grasping his brother's heel as he emerges. Esau is described as red and hairy, hence his name.[25f]

Genesis 25 continued

Esau is a hunter and outdoorsman, while Jacob seems to be something of a homebody and mama's boy. [25g] Isaac loves wild game and naturally favors Esau, who would also be first in line to inherit Isaac's estate. This is his "birthright."

Our first sample of Jacob's dubious moral protocol comes some years later when the two boys have reached an unspecified point in early adulthood.[25h] Jacob is home cooking lentil stew when Esau comes in from hunting with a man-sized hunger. He demands some of the red stew from his brother, who stipulates that Esau first sell him his birthright in payment for the meal.

Esau reasons, perhaps shortsightedly, that he is so hungry that he is about to die anyway, therefore his birthright is useless. Without further thought, Esau swears an oath to Jacob forsaking his birthright, earning him some bread and stew.[25i] The text concludes that Esau despised his birthright.

GENESIS 25 NOTES (continued):

25f. The meaning of Esau's name is clearly explained in the Gen. 25 text ("hairy"), but the meaning of Jacob's name is not. Hebrew scholars concur that "Jacob" indeed means "he who grasps the heel", which is an idiomatic expression meaning one who supplants by treachery or "he who deceives." This is not an auspicious moniker for the man who will give his name to the Israelite people, but it may be an indication of why God renames him after the famous wrestling match (Gen. 32).

25g. Talmudic interpretations of this event are even more detailed, as Talmudic interpretations tend to be. In later Jewish writings, Jacob is understood to be a student. If that is the case, *what was he studying?* God didn't dictate the Torah (Pentateuch) to Moses (including Genesis) for at least five hundred more years!

25h. It is unspecified in the text, but a little backtracking reveals the boys are fifteen.

25i. Lentils, Edom and Esau: The text tells us that hairy Esau was also called Edom, which means red. The color is purported to be related to the lentils in the stew and is also associated with the red rock found in Edom, the land his descendants will inhabit.

GENESIS 26 NOTES:

26a. In light of the amazingly long lifespans of the Patriarchal era, there is no reason not to believe this is the same Abimelech who was in a brief love triangle involving Isaac's Mom and Dad. Considering the biblical emphasis on genealogy, if this king was the son of the Abimelech of Gen. 20, it would likely be mentioned.

26b. In what situation do we imagine Abimelech sitting in a window overlooking Isaac and Rebekah making out? Since Isaac lived in tents, where exactly was the King? Although it is easy to skip these curious details, sometimes they turn out to be important later. In this case, they merely make us knit our eyebrows. One explanation is that Abimelech represents the more urban civilizations already established in the area and Isaac was more or less "camped out" just outside the walls of a city the King controlled.

26c. Gerar and the Valley of Gerar are the same place. The text contradicts itself so many times in this brief passage that we simply need to move on.

26d. This proven success formula had worked well for Abraham before him.

26e. This is another "it's-not-you-it's-the-Bible" moment. Not only has Abraham already dug a well here (Gen. 21), he has also (along with his pal Abimelech) named the place Beersheba. The historical Beersheba was historically founded around 1,000 B.C. and is today the "capital of the Negev."

Genesis 26

Isaac experiences several events and themes paralleling previously recounted incidents in Abraham's life, the most disturbing of which is the habit of passing off his wife as his sister. Esau makes bad marriage decisions and God continues to promote the covenant.

[KJV 889] TSB 432: *Your Savings 457*

Another famine arises, but God tells Isaac not to go down to Egypt this time. Instead, Isaac travels to Gerar in the vicinity of long lived king Abimelech, an old business associate of his father's.[26a] God takes the opportunity to reference his covenant with Abraham for a seventh time, mentioning once again the gift of the land where Isaac is currently sojourning.

Here, Isaac deploys an old trick of his Dad's by introducing his comely wife Rebekah as his sister. Perhaps lacking the powerful allure of mother-in-law Sarah, Isaac's wife doesn't draw immediate marriage proposals. It is only later, when the King is looking down from a convenient window and sees Isaac caressing his wife/sister that he figures out the deception.[26b]

Again, the King's reaction is remarkably even handed. All he does is issue the commandment that anyone who molests Isaac or his wife will be put to death. It isn't until Isaac's crops and superior livestock skills make the local Philistines envious that trouble begins. They fill in the wells that Abraham had dug during his previous sojourn, and shortly thereafter Abimelech tells Isaac to leave.

Isaac moves from Gerar to the Valley of Gerar[26c] and his men begin opening up the wells that have been filled in. They also dig some new wells and discover fresh water, but the herdsmen continue quarreling until Isaac finally digs a third well. This one he calls Rehoboth, which means something like "room enough".

Having apparently solved the water supply issue, he inexplicably moves on to Beersheba, about thirty kilometers south. God appears again and delivers a mercifully short synopsis of the covenant, his eighth. In response, Isaac builds an altar and has his servants begin digging another well.[26d]

Out of the blue, Abimelech shows up with his advisor and commander and wants to make another treaty. According to the King, this request is because they have seen that the Lord is with Isaac. So Isaac has a feast and in the morning they all swear another oath. Later the same day, Isaac's servants show up with the great news that they have found water in the well they have just completed digging. Ever since that time, we are told, the town has been called Beersheba.[26e]

We now return to the hairy but hapless Esau, twenty-five years after the birthright incident. At the age of forty, Esau marries not one but two Hittite women: Judith and Basemath. Rebekah and Isaac are most unhappy with these marriages.

Genesis 27

With the help of his Mom, the sixtyish Jacob continues his deceptive ways by stealing Esau's blessing from Isaac. Esau resolves to kill his brother as Rebekah continues to complain about Hittite wives.

[KJV 1262] TSB 895: *Your Savings 367*

At this point in our story, both Esau (and Jacob) are at least sixty years old.[27a] Esau traded away his birthright for lentil stew forty-five years ago and is now married to a couple of Hittites. The local girls are not popular with Mom and Dad. To this point, there are many unanswered questions regarding what has already transpired between the glimmer twins and there will be many more in this chapter. Just because they are unanswered, however, doesn't mean they aren't relevant. For example, what were the short term consequences of Jacob's original birthright swindle?[27b] Did Jacob mention it in passing to Isaac, and how did his father react? Did Esau brood about giving up his birthright and try to get it back? Complain to Dad? What defined the relationship between the two brothers after the incident? It has been over four decades since the birthright heist: it's hard to imagine there wasn't some tension from time to time at family get-togethers.

We have no answers to these questions as Gen. 27 opens, but are rather informed that Isaac had become old and that his eyes are weak - an important detail as it turns out. Anticipating his death, Isaac summons his favorite son Esau and sends him out to kill some wild game. Esau is to cook up some of the savory food his Dad likes in preparation for receiving his blessing.[27c]

As luck would have it, Rebekah is listening to this conversation and decides to divert the blessing to *her* favorite son: Jacob "the Deceiver". She quickly formulates a devious plan worthy of a Gilbert and Sullivan farce. She tells Jacob to bring two goats from the flock (no time for hunting) so she can prepare a meal of fake wild game for her husband. Posing as Esau, Jacob will take the food to Isaac, and score the blessing instead of Esau.

Jacob proves to be his mother's son by anticipating a problem with her sting strategy: Esau is hairy, but Jacob is a smoother kind of guy, both in terms of skin texture and modus operandi. His concerns are expressed beautifully once again in KJV language: *"My father peradventure will feel me, and I shall seem to him as a deceiver; and I shall bring a curse upon me, and not a blessing".* [27d]

Rebekah says she will accept the curse if they get caught: meanwhile, do what she says. Once the food is prepared, she finds some of Esau's clothes and dresses Jacob in them.[27e] She also covers Jacob's body with the hairy goatskins so his skin will feel rough like his brother's.

GENESIS 27 NOTES:

27a. The Bible doesn't give us Isaac's age, but Jewish writers set his age at 123 and Martin Luther thought it was 137 at this point.

27b. The meaning of the birthright would have been clearly understood by a Hebrew reader, even though in terms of this particular narrative chronology, Mosaic law won't be given until many hundreds of years in the future. As opposed to the blessing that Jacob steals in this chapter, the birthright was a more or less formal economic instrument. When a father died, his male children would be counted and one more number would be added to the count. The inheritance would then be divided by the new total, and the eldest son (or he whom controlled the birthright) would be given two of the portions. To the sixth century B.C writers of Genesis, this law would be a fact of daily life.

27c. The blessing, on the other hand, was an indication of whom the father chose to be the family leader. It would usually fall to the eldest son, but if they messed up it could be changed. Jacob will invoke this traditional exception for his eldest son Reuben in Gen. 49.

27d. In addition to the fact that Jacob shows no particular concern for the immorality of the scam, he uses the phrase "seem to be a deceiver". There is no "seem to be" about it: He is a deceiver. His primary concern here is not that he is hoodwinking his older brother again, but rather that he will be caught and cursed.

27e. To make this Bible story come to life, place yourself in this scene and picture ninety-five year old Rebekah dressing sixty year old Jacob. *Mom! These skins are itchy!*

True Scripture

GENESIS 27 NOTES (continued):

27f. Compare to Abraham's lie in Gen.22 about the Lord providing a sacrifice.

27g. During the conversation with a man/boy he believes is Esau, there is no mention of the purloined birthright, suggesting that Isaac still doesn't know about it at this point. As far as Isaac knows, Esau has just been given the blessing but not the economic benefits of the birthright.

27h. It is curious that the blessing is seen as a literal and almost magical legal instrument, which apparently can't be revoked or revised even if given under false pretences.

27i. This never happens. The brothers lead completely separate lives hundreds of miles away from each other, with Jacob living in mortal fear of his brother's revenge.

27j. A puzzling thing to say since Isaac hasn't died and won't for twenty more years.

27k. Among the many things not revealed in this chapter, Rebekah doesn't appear to remember whose idea the subterfuge was, nor is there mention of any attempt on Isaac's part to remedy the blessing swindle. Although he is initially angry, his prevailing reaction seems to be one of resignation, as if there is nothing to be done about Jacob's crime.

27l. There is a connection between Jacob's escape to Haran in the next chapter and this complaint about the local "daughters of Heth". See more, 28a.

Genesis 27 continued

Jacob takes the savory meat and bread into Isaac and tells him he is Esau, probably lowering his voice a little. He invites his father to eat some of the game (goat) and bestow his blessing. Isaac seems a bit suspicious at first, if only because the "hunting trip" was accomplished so quickly. Jacob (the faux Esau) explains that the Lord provided his success.[27f] After touching Jacob to make sure he is hairy, he asks him one more time if he is Esau and Jacob lies again.

After eating the "game" and drinking some wine, Isaac asks Jacob for a kiss. Noting that Jacob smells like Esau (due to the pasted on goat skins), Isaac delivers the blessing.[27g] The blessing includes this prophecy: not only should his brothers bow down to Jacob, but so should a number of unidentified nations.

Exit Jacob and enter Esau with the tasty meal of wild game he has killed and cooked for his Dad. Naturally, Isaac is confused and asks Esau who he is. The ruse is quickly discovered, causing Isaac to tremble in anger. He tells Esau that unfortunately, the blessing has already been given out.[27h] Nevertheless, Esau bursts out in anger and laments the theft of both his birthright and his blessing. There is no indication either way whether the original birthright incident is news to Isaac at this point.

Esau prevails on his father for what amounts to a leftover blessing and Isaac delivers the bad news in matter of fact terms. He has already made Jacob lord over Esau in addition to giving him all the financial benefits, so what does Esau expect him to do at this point? This doesn't help Esau's frame of mind, so Isaac continues on with a secondary blessing or prophecy, however you wish to view it. While on the one hand Esau is going to dwell in a less than desirable location, legally under the authority of his brother, he will eventually throw off the "yoke."[27i]

This doesn't seem to mollify Esau, who plans to kill Jacob after the days of mourning for Isaac have passed.[27j] Although he is described as saying these words to himself, the walls of these tents have ears and Rebekah hears of his comment. She calls Jacob and suggests he spend some quality time with her brother Laban back in Haran (Mesopotamia/Syria). According to her instructions, Jacob can return when Esau forgets what Jacob has done to him. *"Why should I lose both of you in one day?"* she asks rhetorically?[27k]

In the midst of all this drama, Rebekah takes the opportunity to complain again about Esau's Hittite wives.[27l] If Jacob also goes down that marriage path, she tells Isaac, life just won't be worth living.

Although we may wonder at this point what happened to the sweet virgin who offered to water a servant's camels, there are arguments from Christian and Jewish apologists that seek to justify Rebekah's actions. These interpretations are based on Rebekah's conversation with God while pregnant with the twins, in which He indicates that the older brother will serve the younger. Therefore, Rebekah's engineering of the blessing scam is done in order to keep her husband from contravening the Lord's will. We proceed with the story never knowing whether or not Rebekah thought to tell her husband Isaac about that key conversation with God.

Genesis 28

After more issues with wives, we are treated to the "Jacob's ladder" story of gospel hymn fame. At the top of the ladder, God promises Jacob the land for the ninth time.

[KJV 621] TSB 318: *Your Savings 303*

At the urging of his wife and following the same pattern as Abraham before him, Isaac takes steps to prevent Jacob from marrying locally. He sends Jacob back to Rebekah's brother in Paddan Aram (Haran) to find another Syrian wife.[28a] He re-blesses Jacob and repeats an excerpt from God's promise about the divine but elusive land grant.[28b]

In the first indication that Esau is paying attention, he realizes that his parents disapprove of his Hittite wives. He therefore marries Mahalath, a daughter of his uncle Ishmael.[28c]

On his journey to Haran, Jacob stops for the night at Luz[28d] and uses a stone for a pillow.[28e] This may or may not be the cause of his unusual dream; either way, the vision he has that night makes it easily into the dream hall of fame. He sees a ladder that reaches from earth to heaven, and at the top, presiding over a parade of angels ascending and descending, is the Lord. God announces the covenant details specifically and personally to Jacob for the first time, and for the ninth time overall.

Temporarily in a state of awe, the dream seems to start Jacob on the road to moral and spiritual betterment. Jacob concludes that he has slept right at the gate of Heaven and that he is in the presence of God. He sets the stone upright, anoints it with oil, and changes the name of the city from Luz to Bethel.[28f]

However, by way of demonstrating that his ethical rehabilitation is not yet complete, he makes a "business vow", which is something of a conditional agreement with God. His deal with God requires that the deity watch over him and give him safe passage back home, at which point he will give God back a tenth of whatever God gives him.[28g] If God holds up his end, the stone pillar will be his house.[28h]

GENESIS 28 NOTES:

28a. A return to the clan's homeland in western Mesopotamia.

28b. The narrative contains no description of Isaac remonstrating with Jacob or Rebekah concerning their deception.

28c. Considering Ishmael's tainted lineage, it is never clear that this is regarded as an upgrade.

28d. If Jacob made it to Luz, then he was outside of a good-sized city. The gates of cities were closed at sundown, so he would have had to sleep out of doors.

28e. Over the millennia, this rock/pillow/pillar has taken on a life of its own. Among the traditions not found in the Bible is the belief that Jacob later set the stone up in Jerusalem. Eventually this amazing stone supposedly traveled to Spain, Ireland and Scotland. For some years, the kings of Scotland were crowned on a stone claimed to be Jacob's pillar. Later, Edward I brought it to Westminster, where it now resides under the chair upon which the king sits during the crowning process.

28f. Bethel or Beth-El means house (Beth) of God (El). Think of El as a nickname for Elohim. In the Bible, the Patriarchs never consult with the residents when they rename a place. In this case, it appears that the locals went along with the renaming.

28g. God could then deduct the 10% and provide Jacob with the net proceeds.

28h. More or less "home away from home" whenever God is in Beth-El.

GENESIS 29 NOTES:

29a The parallels between the well scene involving Abraham's servant and Rebekah should be obvious. There are also key differences.

29b. Laban would be Jacob's uncle on his mother's side.

29c. Rachel means "ewe" (a female lamb), implying Jacob's well known sheepherding skills operate metaphorically on several levels. She would also be Jacob's first cousin.

29d. The comparison between the sisters is interesting, as the strength of Rachel's eyesight is not discussed, nor is Leah's appearance expressly dealt with. Nevertheless, it is made clear in a rather nuanced way that Leah is not a Bible babe.

29e. Although it seems unlikely that Jacob would not know with whom he is consummating his marriage, it is perhaps not as implausible as it might seem to a modern Western reader. It remains the custom in some eastern countries for the bridegroom to go to bed first. The veiled bride is brought to him in the dark, so if he's been celebrating the wedding excessively he may not know the difference. Ironically, this switcheroo echoes Jacob's own epic substitution many decades in the past.

Genesis 29

Jacob's search for a wife parallels that of his father until Laban the Syrian (Aramean) opens a big can of karmic payback by deceiving the deceiver. Nevertheless, Jacob's first wife makes a good start producing the twelve tribes.

[KJV 849] TSB 647: *Your Savings 202*

When Jacob gets to Haran he encounters three flocks of sheep near a water well capped by a large stone.[29a] Jacob asks the nearby shepherds where they are from, if they know Laban and if he is well.[29b] Jacob, presaging his soon to be revealed livestock management skills, wants to water the sheep and return them to pasture. Unfortunately, there is some sort of local policy that requires all of the flocks to be present before the stone can be rolled away.

About this time, who should happen along but Laban's daughter, the comely shepherdess Rachel.[29c] Policy or not, Jacob rolls away the stone and waters Laban's sheep, a task with which he will become all too familiar. Kissing his nice looking cousin and weeping, he tells her who he is. She runs to tell her father about the visitor.

Laban, perhaps recalling the excellent gifts born by Abraham's servant many decades past, hurries right out to meet Jacob. Thus begins the tale of a complex, sometimes mutually beneficial, sometimes abusive relationship between Jacob and his father-in-law. Having journeyed here to escape the anger of his brother, the Patriarch in training now begins a prolonged stay working for Laban. After a month, Laban offers Jacob the opportunity to set his own pay, which Jacob quickly suggests should be Laban's daughter Rachel. He thinks seven years labor is a reasonable payment for Rachel's hand and the men seal the deal.

We already know that Rachel is a fine looking woman, but now we find out she has an older sister Leah, a woman with weak eyes.[29d] This becomes a problem when Jacob's seven years of servitude have expired, at which point he tells Laban that his part of the deal is completed and he is anxious to have sex with Rachel. This is more information than most potential sons-in-law are likely to share with their future fathers-in-law, but this is the Bible and Laban hosts the wedding feast, albeit with a "slight" change of plans. After the feast, Jacob awaits his new bride in his tent. It is not until the cold light of dawn that he notices he has bedded Leah instead of Rachel.[29e] What the…?

Genesis 29 continued

Jacob realizes he has been hoodwinked, and (considering his own history of deceptions) he self-righteously takes the matter up with his new father-in-law. Unrepentant, Laban decides this is the time to share local marriage policy, which is that the oldest daughter has to be married first. But he makes Jacob another deal: all Jacob has to do is finish out his wedding week duties and then he can own Rachel too. Oh, yes: he will also owe Laban an additional seven years of labor. To show he's a stand up guy, Laban is willing to pay up front for the next installment of Jacob's herd management skills. During the festivities, Laban also awards two handmaidens to his newly married daughters. Rachel gets Bilhah and Leah gets Zilpah.[29f] We will hear more about these two.

Suddenly husband to two wives, Jacob finds that he loves Rachel but not the weak-eyed Leah. This situation is an affront to God's peculiar sense of fairness, so he decides to even the competitive playing field by making Leah fertile and Rachel barren.[29g] However Jacob feels about his first wife, he mans up and performs his husbandly chores as Leah starts cranking out the first four forebears of the twelve tribes of Israel. The first child Reuben is so named because God has backed Leah, which she hopes will earn her Jacob's love. It doesn't, but she continues to hope as she produces Simeon, Levi and Judah in short order.[29h] The weak eyes are no problem when it comes to childbearing.

At this point, Leah's birthing marathon runs out of fuel and other women prepare to step up to the plate with eight tribes to go.

29f. Zilpah means "drooping" and Bilhah means "faltering" or "bashful." Jewish tradition has them as half-sisters, daughters of Laban's concubine. They may or may not have been slaves, as the distinction was less clear cut in ancient societies. One of these women will cost Reuben his birthright and it won't be because she is bashful.

29g. It's never certain what is going to influence God's barometer of justice. He doesn't seem to worry too much about Hagar's problems, yet Leah's marital issues cause him to bestow a fertility upgrade on her.

29h. Reuben means "behold, a son". Simeon means "to hear or be heard". The names are derived from the Hebrew verbs to see and to hear. Levi is derived from the word "attach", because Leah believes that now Jacob will become attached to her.

For his part, Judah's name is the source of the term "Jew". The English Judah is derived from Yehuda, which in turn is probably derived from JHWH (Jahweh, Yahweh, Jehovah, etc.), the other Old Testament God name with the ambiguous vowels. It can also mean "praise." JHWH doesn't formally introduce himself by that name until Exodus 3.

We will see why it is Leah's fourth child rather than Reuben who gives his name to the historically dominant tribe.

GENESIS 30 NOTES:

30a. Dan means "judging" because Rachel feels she has been judged favorably by God. It is significant that Rachel names the child rather than Bilhah.

30b. Naphtali in Hebrew means something like "my wrestling", because Rachel feels she has wrestled with her sister and won (nevertheless, Leah has doubled Rachel's output despite the latter's recruitment of slave labor).

30c. Gad means "troop" in Hebrew, but the reference is unclear.

30d. Asher means "happy".

30e. Mandrakes were thought to improve fertility.

30f. But it might have been something like "you did what?" One does wonder about the administration of Jacob's (and anyone else in a polygamous marriage scenario for that matter) nightly bed partner schedule. Is it a calendar, a lottery or a free for all? Why is Rachel able to barter a night with the stud muffin Jacob? Is she leasing her regular night to Leah, or has the weak eyed one been marginalized in the sexual sweepstakes?

30g. Meaning "a hire". This connotation is clear, although it may have made Jacob feel cheap.

30h. Zebulun means "a dwelling."

Genesis 30

The sisters continue their breeding competition through surrogates and Jacob outsmarts his unethical father-in-law with divinely inspired cattle breeding techniques.

[KJV 1022] TSB 596: *Your Savings 426*

With Leah out-breeding her four to nothing, Rachel complains to Jacob and threatens to die if he doesn't get her some kids. He becomes a bit outraged that she is expecting Godlike powers from him and makes it clear that it is God that *"hath withheld from thee the fruit of the womb"*. [KJV]

Reprising Sarah's ill fated plan from back in Gen. 22, Rachel decides Jacob should sleep with her slave girl, reasoning that if Bilhah gives birth on Rachel's lap, then it will count as a legitimate substitution. This plan is put in effect, and the result is tribal leader number five, whom Rachel names Dan.[30a] Bilhah comes through again and delivers Naphtali.[30b]

Concerned that Rachel/Bilhah are closing the breeding gap, Leah gives Jacob her "droopy" slave/maid and she bears Gad[30c] and Asher.[30d]

The trouble between the sisters escalates as Rachel asks Leah to give her some of the mandrake roots Reuben has found in a wheat field.[30e] Leah bitterly asks Rachel if taking away her husband isn't enough. By way of bartering for the mandrakes, Rachel tells Leah she can sleep with Jacob that night. Leah goes so far as to inform Jacob he's on for the night because she has bought a night of his attentions from Rachel. Jacob's response is not recorded.[30f]

As luck would have it though, Leah not only gets a romp with her husband but is impregnated to boot: the child Issachar will grow up to be forebear of tribe number nine.[30g] Apparently she was invited back for an encore, because next thing we know she is giving birth to Zebulun and then to a daughter Dinah.[30h] Dinah does not get a tribe of her own, but she does provoke the massacre of a major city in Gen. 34.

Genesis 30 continued

Finally, God "remembers" Rachel and gives her a child of her own: Joseph.[30i]

Growing weary of working for his father-in-law, Joseph asks Laban to release him to return to his own country. Laban is reluctant to let him go, acknowledging that his own wealth has increased because of Jacob's excellent relationship with God. When Laban asks him what he wants in order to stay on as manager, Jacob asks only for the spotted or speckled goats and the brown sheep from Laban's herd.

Ever the chiseler, Laban removes all the spotted cattle and brown sheep from his herd and has his sons hide them from Jacob. But Jacob makes use of some tree branches to game the breeding process, peeling back the bark to expose strips of white underneath. He sets these branches up by the watering troughs as a white and dark visual cue for the animals to gaze upon while mating. This subliminal suggestion causes the dams and cows to conceive a high percentage of speckled and spotted offspring.[30j] According to his agreement with Laban, all of this multicolored livestock belongs to Jacob. Jacob performs further do-it-yourself genetic engineering by placing the striped rods only near the strongest cattle when they are breeding. Keeping his duotone livestock separated from Laban's, he ends up with all the robust sheep and cattle, while Laban's unblemished livestock is feeble.

Here we finally get a glimpse of why the Lord has picked Jacob as the namesake-to-be of the chosen people. Not only does he display stamina in performing his husbandly duties, but his husbandry talents are innovative and effective. In this manner he builds his wealth, including maid servants, man servants and camels, in addition to his cattle.

GENESIS 30 NOTES (continued):

30i. In Hebrew, "adding".

30j. The people and deities of the Bible are deeply concerned with the aesthetic quality of livestock.

True Scripture

GENESIS 31 NOTES:

31a. Jacob should be about eighty at this point, perhaps old enough to free himself from his uncle's influence.

31b. This is a slightly muddled version that involves male goats, but the breeding results are the same.

31c. It is interesting that Laban worships idols. Recall that Rebekah sends Jacob back to her homeland because she doesn't want him to marry an idol worshipping Hittite woman. But ironically enough, her own brother Laban (Rachel's father) keeps idols in the house. Now we ask: Has Rachel stolen these "gods" out of spite, or because she wants to worship them?

31d. Gilead is a mountainous region just East of the Jordan River. It means "hill of testimony" or "mound of witness".

31e. A little unfair, considering that Jacob has labored for a total of fourteen years and bought the girls fair and square. The deal was not a "rent to own" agreement.

31f. Laban's language makes it clear that the deity who contacted him was the "God of your father." This god was not Laban's god (hence the idols), nor even necessarily Jacob's God.

31g. No one likes a god stealer.

31h. That's right. Time to pull out your Bible and verify for yourself. Your Sunday School teacher skipped this part?

Genesis 31

There are some awkward moments concerning stolen idols as Jacob tries to sneak home to Canaan[31a] and Laban catches up with him in Gilead.

[KJV 1022] TSB 596: *Your Savings 426*

God tells Jacob he wants him to return to Canaan, not a bad idea since Laban and his sons have become hostile to him over unresolved livestock issues. Jacob calls his wives together and tells them a version of the "striped and speckled livestock" story. In Jacob's version, slightly altered from Gen. 30, it is God whom has intervened in the mating process on Jacob's behalf, because Laban has tried to cheat Jacob again, changing his wages no fewer than ten times.[31b] The net result is that Jacob now owns all Laban's livestock due to God's intervention. This situation was all explained to Jacob by an angel (he tells his daughters), speaking for God in the first person via a dream. Noting further that Jacob has his full support because of the vow he made at the Bethel stone/pillar, the angel/God told Jacob he had better get out of town.

As Rachel and Leah see it, their father Laban already views them as foreigners and has gladly spent the proceeds gotten from selling his daughters to Jacob. As far as they're concerned, their husband should go ahead and follow God's instructions.

No stranger to abrupt departures, Jacob gathers everyone and everything and leaves Paddan-Aram (Haran) without saying goodbye. Unfortunately, prior to departure Rachel has stolen her father's household idols while he is out sheering his flock (as opposed to fleecing Jacob).[31c] Unaware of this theft, Jacob crosses the Euphrates and heads toward Gilead.[31d]

For whatever reason, it takes Laban three days to notice that Jacob and all the livestock have left the area. After a week, Laban overtakes Jacob's party at Gilead. Upon his arrival, God tells Laban in a dream he should *"take heed that thou speak not to Jacob either good or bad."* [KJV] We can see why Jacob's father-in-law wasn't selected by God to be a Patriarch because as soon as he finds Jacob, Laban ignores God's warning, issuing some fairly unpleasant commentary concerning deception and the theft of his daughters.[31e] Furthermore, Laban claims his feelings are hurt because he would have wanted to throw a nice going away party. Switching tones yet again, he tells Jacob that he might even have done him harm, if God hadn't warned him off.[31f] Finally, Laban suggests that he can put all the rest of this behind him, but the one thing he simply can't get over is the theft of his gods.[31g]

Genesis 31 continued

Not knowing his favorite wife is the guilty party, Jacob promises whoever has stolen the idols "will not live." All the tents are searched, but to no avail because Rachel has hidden them in her camel's saddlebag. Sitting on the idols, she demonstrates that she has learned a few things from her trickster Dad and husband. She tells her father than she can't rise in his presence because she is having her period.[31h]

Laban's failure to find the idols triggers a Jacobean whiny tirade that unleashes all the frustration of the past twenty years.[31i] While it's hard to blame him, Jacob has been harboring a laundry list of injustices done him by Laban, a large percentage of which have to do with livestock. He concludes the rant by pointing out that the God of his parents has sided with *him* throughout the ordeal, hence his track record of pastoral innovation.

Laban doesn't seem entirely convinced, but he offers to make a covenant for the good of the family.[31j] Falling back on his default behavior, Jacob immediately sets up a stone as a pillar, then has his kinsmen heap more stones around it. After while, they all have a happy meal there by the stone heap. Although the covenant is now in effect, Laban and Jacob show they are still not on the same page by naming the place differently. Laban calls it *Jegar-sahadutha*, but Jacob names it *Galeed* and *Mitzpah*.[31k] In spite of the controversy, we are left with an excellent Bible verse, spoken by Laban to Jacob: *"The LORD watch between you and me when we are absent one from the other."* [KJV] Although children are taught this verse as a poetic and affectionate parting phrase, it is in fact quite the opposite. The stone heap has actually been placed there to remind each of them that God[31l] is watching their moves to make sure they don't break the treaty, and further, that neither is permitted to pass the new landmark for the purpose of harming the other.[31m]

Jacob swears to the truce and throws another banquet. In the morning, Laban kisses the kids and everyone goes their way.

GENESIS 31 NOTES (continued):

31i. Although Karma isn't heavily spotlighted in the Bible (Buddha won't be born for more than a thousand years), it's hard not to see some "what goes around come around" blowback here for "he who grasps the heel".

31j. This covenant anticipates a later event in the same location that initiates the Hebrew monarchy.

31k. Jegar-sahadutha and Galeed both mean "an heap of witness" but in different but similar dialects. Laban, speaks Chaldean / Syrian while Jacob, although only two generations removed from Mesopotamia, now speaks "Hebrew".

Mitzpah means watchtower.

31l. Laban continues to acknowledge that it will be Jacob's family god acting as referee, possibly because someone has stolen his. Because the concept of monotheism was a radical idea even when this material was written down in the seventh - sixth century B.C., Laban's language throughout these chapters suggests that he regards Jacob's god as one among many, albeit one with some juice.

31m. One of the conditions of the agreement is that Jacob should not marry other wives in addition to Laban's daughters (slave handmaidens don't count). It is of interest that Laban considers the taking of additional wives other than his own daughters to be a breach of trust. It is difficult to distinguish between filial love and his attitude that they are also his property to be sold.

GENESIS 32 NOTES:

32a. The name is "Mahanaim", which means "God's camp" or "two camps."

32b. That's what the Genesis text says. But a quick glance at the map on page 4 shows that Jacob wouldn't have had to go anywhere near Edom to get to Canaan from Haran or Gilead.

32c. A tributary of the Jordan, joining it some 30 Km north of the Dead Sea.

32d. If Jacob is tough enough to beat God in marathon wrestling, it is puzzling that he's afraid of his brother. Furthermore, after all of His talk about being the creator of the universe, it's disappointing that Elohim can't out-grapple Jacob. One possibility is that Jacob's numerous wives and concubines have helped him keep his all night wrestling skills tuned up.

32e. In the absence of clear guidance, we are given to understand that God can't beat Jacob fairly, so He has to cheat by using His divine power to dislocate his thigh. We are never told how this injury heals., but there is other guy to guy thigh touching in Genesis.

32f. The the exact meaning of the Hebrew word "Israel" is tricky (just like the former Jacob). Hebrew is an ancient Semitic language of Canaan, and El began his global career as the Canaanite Father God. In this context, it is clear that the "El" part of Isra-el refers to the ancient Canaanite/Hebrew God. The ambiguous component is the "Isra". This part of the word is a verb form which may mean "struggles", but could also mean "dominates" or "rules". So "Israel" might mean anything along an etymological continuum from "Struggles with God" to "God Rules."

32g. Peni-el means "face of God". Note again the "El" component at the end.

Genesis 32

After some embarrassingly obsequious behavior on Jacob's part vis a vis Esau, he sends his family and herds on ahead while he spends the night wrestling. Ultimately, this night of manly roughhousing pays off in the form of a blessing...and a whole new name.

[KJV 794] TSB 453: *Your Savings 341*

After a brief meeting with a couple of angels who are on an undisclosed mission, Jacob originates yet another place name[32a], then realizes he has to deal with his brother Esau in order to pass through Edom (Seir).[32b] He sends emissaries with a sycophantic message to his brother, along with gifts on the hoof, plus some servants. He is seeking, of course, to find favor in the eyes of "my Lord", as he now addresses his twin.

The messengers return with the news that Esau is on his way to meet Jacob with four hundred men. With no clear indication as to whether Esau is planning revenge or whether the four hundred men just want to shake his hand, Jacob takes steps to cut his losses. He divides his family and herds in half: should Esau attack one group, the other may escape. Leaving nothing to chance, he reminds God that he is returning home on His instructions and asks for protection from his brother. This time, he reminds God about the covenant between them rather than the other way around.

Finally, Jacob ups the ante with an additional gift of hundreds of goats, ewes, rams, camels and donkeys, making sure the servants drive the animals ahead where Esau can see the gift herd. Jacob reiterates that he is all about appeasing Esau. He sends his wives and children across the Jabbok river and spends the night alone.[32c]

Well, not exactly alone, as the next thing we know he is wrestling the night away with a mysterious Man. Although Jacob and the whole rest of the Abrahamic family seem to dream vividly, this wrestling match is not characterized as a dream. The Man who is probably God can't seem to beat the wily herdsman[32d], so he dislocates Jacob's thigh.[32e] Parenthetically, we are informed that modern Israelites don't eat the hip sinew because God touched it. This aside is another clue as to whom Jacob was wrestling.

He (the Man) asks Jacob to let him go, but Jacob insists the Man bless him first as a condition. The Man first asks Jacob's name, then changes it to Israel, which is commonly said to mean "you have striven with God and men and have prevailed."[32f]

That's an impressive moniker for the Chosen People, or any other people for that matter. From this point forward, we are dealing with the Israelites, Jacob's descendants, so named as the result of a wrestling match.

The Man declines to give Jacob his own name when asked, but he does bless him. Jacob names the place Peniel.[32g] At dawn, nursing his thigh wound, Jacob limps across the river to meet his brother Esau after twenty years of uncomfortable separation.

Genesis 33

The freshly named but still crafty Israel (Jacob) meets up with his forgiving but still gullible brother and tells him one last fib.

[KJV 794] TSB 453: *Your Savings 341*

Having been up all night wrestling and now limping from his injury, Jacob/Israel looks ahead and sees Esau coming with his small army. He divides the children among their four mothers. Ranking them in reverse order, he puts the maids and their children in the front[33a], then Leah with her seven children[33b], and finally Rachel with Joseph bringing up the rear. Jacob/Israel goes on ahead and bows down seven times as Esau arrives.[33c]

Esau and Jacob/Israel have a nice, tearful reunion, with Jacob/Israel's kids and wives all bowing as they are introduced to their uncle.[33d] At first the elder twin declines all the cattle and livestock, but he eventually allows himself to be persuaded by Jacob/Israel's fawning importuning.

Esau suggests they travel together and offers to guide the company, but Jacob/Israel declines, explaining that he doesn't want to push the kids and flocks too hard. He tells Esau they will catch up to him at Seir.[33e] Right. After offering to leave some servants as guides, Esau returns home. But wily Jacob/Israel does not go south to Seir as promised.[33f] Instead he travels west and stops for a time at Sukkoth, where he builds a house for himself and "booths" for his cattle.[33g]

At an unspecified time after building this house and these booths, he travels further west to a new location at Shechem and sets up his camp outside the city.[33h]

He purchases some land from the city boss, Hamor[33i] and builds an altar called El-Elohe-Israel.[33j]

Although he has traveled *west* to get to this place, events are about to go *south* in a big way.

William Tyndale's 1537 English translation of the Septuagint describes this event as follows: *"And Iacob went to Salem to ye cytie of Sichem in the lande of Canaa after that'he was come from Mesopotamia and pitched before the cyte."*

GENESIS 33 NOTES:

33a. Up front in harms way would be Zilpah and Bilhah, along with their children Dan, Naphtali, Gad and Asher.

33b. Leah's seven children are Reuben, Simeon, Levi and Judah, Issachar, Zebulon and Dinah.

33c. Even though his birthright and blessing are ill-gotten, Jacob nevertheless technically outranks Esau. Protocol should require that Esau bow to him.

33d. Most people would have mentioned that they had just been up all night grabbling with El, and oh by the way, call me Israel now. That's what my new best friend God calls me.

33e. Seir is the hill country of Edom, located south of the Dead Sea. Over the course of the next several centuries, Esau's kin will develop into the Edomites, another major enemy waiting to greet the Chosen People after their stay in Egypt.

33f. He may have gotten a brand new name from God, but the old deceiver seems to be alive and well.

33g. He calls this place Succoth, which means "booths" or "huts". Succoth is now a Jewish festival which involves building temporary shelters, but does not commemorate this particular event.

33h. We have already encountered Shechem as the location of Abraham's first altar and the recurring oak tree. As you read the next chapter, bear in mind that Shechem is also the name of the young prince, son of Hamor (or Emmor) the headman of the city of. Otherwise, it might be confusing.

33i. Hamor the Hivite. As with many of the local tribes, the Hivites are also Canaanites.

33j. Recall that back in Gen. 12, Abraham built his first altar in this area. The El word is embedded in the name of the latest altar three times. It translates as "El, the God of Israel", or "God, the God of the God who struggles (or rules)".

GENESIS 34 NOTES:

34a. Dinah is understood to be 13 - 15 years of age. This means either Israel spent some years amongst the booths at Succoth before he moved on, or that he was in Shechem for a while before Dinah decided to step out.

34b. After more than three millennia, the interpretation of this text is all over the map. One thing that seems clear: whether this encounter was rape or mutual consent is immaterial to the brothers back in camp.

34c. After the name change, Israel's offspring are the Israelites.

34d. Deceptive conduct being inherited from Dad.

Genesis 34

After the feel good interlude in the previous chapter, things begin to unravel in Shechem. Parental discretion is suggested for this chapter as it includes rape, serial killings, grand larceny, deception and mass circumcision.

[KJV 790] TSB 543: *Your Savings 247*

Remember Dinah, the only girl born to Israel's wives and surrogates? As the new girl in Shechem, she decides to go see what the local social scene is all about.[34a] As she is checking out the action, she ends up having sex with young Prince Shechem, son of Hamor, the headman of the city. [34b] To his credit, Shechem conducts himself like a prince and seems to have genuine affection for the lusty young Israelite girl.[34c] Like any normal royal offspring, he asks his Dad to get her as a wife. Hamor heads out to talk to Israel about the "situation."

When Israel hears the story, he keeps it to himself until his sons get home from the fields, at which point there is a confrontation between Hamor and Israel's boys.

Hamor attempts some damage control, and rather convincingly makes a case for a practical resolution to a tricky situation. "Why don't you join forces with us and we can all live as equals?" he suggests graciously. This seems to be a generous resolution of the conflict, especially considering (and this establishes a pattern that lasts several thousand years) the Israelites just arrived in town. Prince Shechem, again seeming to be a straightforward (if lovestruck) young fellow, tells Dinah's family to name a price and let the marriage festivities begin.

In response, Israel's kids answer Hamor in terms which are described explicitly as deceptive.[34d] The problem, as they explain it, is that they can't let their sister marry an uncircumcised man, even if he is a prince. Their terms are that every male in Shechem must undergo the Elohim sanctioned foreskin modification. Under these conditions, they say, the two peoples can intermarry.

Shechem is so enamored of Dinah that he gets God's required penis surgery right on the spot. This decision enhances his prestige among his fellow Hivites, if perhaps reducing his phallic profile to some degree. Hamor and his son then address the men of Shechem concerning their new best friends the Israelites and the economic benefits of circumcision. In what may the only case on record in favor of circumcision as a facilitator of commerce, they paint a glowing picture of the two peoples merging, sharing women and livestock and generally living the good life. Hamor must have been a convincing orator, because all the men of the city immediately line up for the penile alteration.

Genesis 34 continued

Three days after the mass operation, when every man in Shechem is still immobilized by pain, brothers Simeon and Levi attack the city and kill every man in it, including the love smitten Shechem and his indulgent Dad. They take Dinah back to their camp. Israel's other sons loot the city and steal the livestock, widows and kids.

For his part, Israel seems annoyed primarily at the trouble Simeon and Levi have caused him. His concern, at least the part we are told about, is that the other Canaanites in the region are going to take exception to this odious behavior. He is not particularly uneasy about the wholesale slaughter of innocent people, nor the theft of their property. Instead, he notes that his people are way outnumbered in the area. But the sons answer, *"should he treat our sister as a harlot?"*[34e] [KJV]

The chapter ends on that rhetorical note.

GENESIS 34 NOTES (continued):

34e. Although there will be some penalties down the line for Simeon and Levi in Gen. 49, that's pretty much the end of this particular event. The Canaanites come out of this situation looking civilized and reasonable compared to Israel's offspring.

GENESIS 35 NOTES:

35a. Bethel or Beth-El (House of El) is where the Patriarch formerly known as Jacob set up a pillar using the stone upon which his head was resting at the time he had the stairway to heaven dream (Gen. 28). It is south of Shechem.

35b. Again we might consider why Rachel stole her father's idols. Remember, Israel doesn't know she stole them in the first place. Did she pinch them in order to worship them in secret and does she turn them in now?

35c. The tree we have encountered previously, when grandfather Abraham built his first altar. We will encounter it again.

35d. It is hard to imagine what a traveler would have concluded had they come upon the aftermath of the massacre at Shechem. It may not have been clear that the victims were circumcised first and murdered later. To a barbarian Canaanite, it would not be obvious that circumcision was mandated by God.

35e. Meaning "tree of tears." Rebekah's wet nurse is at least hundred-forty years old so she isn't that wet anymore. Why is she traveling with Israel's household? As with so many other aspects of the Bible, there are extra-biblical traditions involving this nurse. Kabbalah, the mystical Hebrew science of numerology says she was later reincarnated as Deborah, the famous judge who led the Jews in a battle against the Canaanites which continues to this very day.

35f. At this point, El-Bethel is beginning to look like Stonehenge.

35g. This place may also be Bethlehem.

35h. "To this day" would mean the sixth B.C. when this material was first composed, also known as the Persian period.

35i. The sudden appearance of Esau, who has journeyed north from Seir, makes one wonder. Isn't he curious as to why Israel never showed back in Gen.33?

Genesis 35

Following God's advice to get out of Shechem, Israel returns to Bethel and builds two more altars. He renames Bethel twice and God reaffirms the covenant for the tenth time. Isaac dies and Esau attends the funeral.

[KJV 664] TSB 445: *Your Savings 219*

Confirming Israel's concerns, God tells him (and not for the first time) he should probably get out of town. Specifically, he should head back to Bethel and make another altar.[35a] Israel therefore gives a pep talk to his people, instructing them to put away their foreign gods and purify themselves. They turn in their god statues and ritual earrings[35b] and Israel hides them under the oak at Shechem.[35c]

As Israel and his household head down to Bethel, we are told that a great terror fell upon the towns in the region, possibly having heard of the recent events in Shechem.[35d] At Bethel he builds another altar and calls it El-Bethel, which literally means God of the House of God.

Here we pause for a jarringly random mention of the death of Rebekah's wet nurse and her burial under an oak called Allon-bacuth.[35e]

Although God has already renamed Jacob, he uses this occasion to rename him Israel again. He then repeats the promises of the covenant for the tenth time and predicts glorious things for the future. He states the following: *"And the land which I gave Abraham and Isaac, to thee I will give it, and to thy seed after thee will I give the land."* [KJV]

Bear in mind that Israel is now in the place where he set up the pillar on his way to Paddan-Aram a couple of decades previously. On that visit he named the place Bethel. Just prior to that one-sided conversation with God (El), he built an altar and called it El-Bethel. Now, he sets up another pillar and pours out a drink offering and then tops it off with some oil.[35f] At this point, he re-renames the place Bethel. With God as a role model, Israel is comfortable repeating himself.

God is not on record as telling Israel to leave, nevertheless we find the tribe on the move again when Rachel goes into difficult childbirth labor. She dies giving birth to Benjamin, Israel's twelfth male child and thirteenth overall. Rachel is buried on the road to Ephrath.[35g] Israel sets up a pillar at the site, which is said to be there "to this day."[35h]

Israel continues moving south toward Hebron. He is camped near the Tower of Eder when he hears that his eldest son Reuben has been sleeping with "bashful" Bilhah, Rachel's handmaiden and mother of his half brothers Dan and Naphtali.

That story line ends abruptly and we are given a synopsis of Israel's children. With that out of the way, Israel visits his father Isaac at Hebron. Isaac dies at the age of one hundred-eighty and his sons Esau and Israel bury him.[35i] Note that Isaac managed to hold on for at least another two decades after he gave his final blessing to Jacob.

Genesis 36

A huge time saver for you the reader as we summarize why the descendants of Esau are important, without having to name all of them.

[KJV 845] TSB 231: *Your Savings 614*

This "Esau interlude" itemizes the descendants of the hairy red guy and is a throwaway chapter in terms of the narrative progression. However, there are items of interest embedded in this material. First recall that Esau in Gen. 26 married two Canaanite women (incurring his Mom's displeasure) and later the daughter of his loser uncle Ishmael. These three wives are noted in Gen. 36 as well, but they are given completely different names than previously. Basemath, originally the offspring of Elon the Hittite, is now the daughter of Ishmael. The other two wives are also named differently and come from different families.

This chapter includes another oddity, a passage that describes Esau moving to Seir because the combination of his livestock and Jacob's were more than the land could support. There is no time frame indicated, so we don't know whether this is supposed to be in the real time of the narrative (after Isaac's death) or instead refers to the incidents of decades past. In this telling, there is no mention of the birthright theft as the reason for both of the lads leaving Beersheba in their sixties.

Esau's progeny are detailed here for several generations, including a number of "dukes" [KJV] or "chiefs" [ASV]. However, the names listed are consistent in many cases with more or less historic Edomite kings associated with traditions of many centuries later.[36a]

GENESIS 36 NOTES:

36a. This supplemental text is widely believed to be an insert into the main text from a different author. Biblical scholars who are not literalists attribute these and many other contradictions to the fact that Bible is comprised of multiple sources. The various legends have been stitched together to form a less than consistent narrative line. Gen. 36 is likely from a source more sympathetic toward the Edomites.

GENESIS 37 NOTES:

37a. Although he has been renamed Israel twice, the narrative continues to call him Jacob most of the time. We will abide by God's wishes and identify him by his new God-given name.

37b. Dan, Naphtali, Gad and Asher.

37c. Joseph is described as Jacob's favorite because he is "the son of his old age". However, Joseph is hardly younger than his other brothers. It is usually understood that he is the favorite because he is Rachel's son.

37d. This is obviously several years after the circumcision massacre.

37e. This group would be their cousins, the second or third generation of their grand uncle Ishmael's offspring.

37f. These same traders are called Midianites in the next paragraph, a discrepancy usually attributed to the splicing of multiple Biblical sources. Midian was Abraham's fourth child by Keturah (Gen. 25), his concubine after Sarah's death. Midianites and Ishmaelites are both cousins of the newly dubbed Israelites. If these were distinct ethnic groups at the time of the story, they were also relatives of Israel's boys. Ishmael is regarded as the father of the Arabic peoples (hence his portrayal as the son of slave).

37g. We aren't told whether or not his brothers tell Reuben the truth.

37h. This is the first mention of an afterlife-related destination in the Bible. Although it is widely understood to be Hell by modern Christian audiences, the ancient Hebrews regarded the concept of Sheol as more or less of a void or abyss. The Greeks translated the word as Hades, which is a quite different vision of the afterlife than either Hell or Sheol. The notion of Hell as a post mortem punishment destination was made up much later by Christians.

Genesis 37

This chapter is the beginning of the concluding Genesis sequence, which sends the Israel family down into Egypt for four hundred years. Joseph, son of Israel's favorite and now dead wife, is the star of this tale. In this chapter, he is sold into slavery, creating the material for a successful musical.

[KJV 942] TSB 502: *Your Savings 440*

With Israel[37a] now living in Hebron, his seventeen year old son Joseph is out in the fields with the offspring of Bilhah and Zilpah.[37b] Our first news of handsome and talented Joseph shows him tattling on his brothers. He is obviously Israel's favorite, but not highly regarded by his siblings.[37c] Contributing to his brothers' hatred of Joseph is the multicolored tunic his Dad has made for him.

Besides being a tattletale, Joseph is socially tone deaf, describing a dream to his brothers guaranteed to make them insecure. In the dream, they are all binding sheaves of grain, but Joseph's sheaf stands up erect while their sheaves bow down to their younger brother's sheaf. The recounting of this dream does not improve the relationship with his brothers, but that doesn't prevent him from sharing the next dream. Just in case we missed the subtleties of the first midnight allegory, the second dream describes the sun, moon and eleven stars bowing down to Joseph. Even Israel doesn't like this dream, as he interprets it as signifying he too might be required to genuflect. In spite of the rebuke he delivers, Israel continues to wonder if the dream has some meaning.

When the other brothers take the flocks north to pasture in Shechem[37d], Israel sends Joseph up to see how they are doing. Apparently lost, he encounters a man who sends him to his brothers in Dothan. As he is approaching, his brothers decide this is a great opportunity to put "the dreamer" (and tattletale) to death. They plan to kill him and throw him in a pit, but Reuben intervenes. He suggests they just throw him in the pit, secretly planning, we are told, to rescue him later. So they confiscate Joseph's tunic and throw him in the hole.

Not particularly concerned with their most recent crime, which is mild compared to the massacre and plunder of Shechem, the brothers sit down to eat. Along comes a caravan of Ishmaelites carrying gum, balm and myrrh on their camels.[37e] Judah has an idea: why kill Joseph and make no money on the deal, when they can sell him to the Ishmaelites for a profit? His observation that Joseph is "of their own flesh" seems disingenuous at this point. So they sell him to the Ishmaelites who might also be Midianites for twenty shekels of silver, and the traders carry him down to Egypt. [37f]

We don't know where Reuben went, but when he gets back to the pit he is really upset to find Joseph gone. He says *"the boy is not there, as for me, where am I to go?"*[37g] Someone decides they should slaughter a goat, dip the tunic in it and take it to Israel. Their Dad naturally concludes that Joseph has been eaten by a wild beast. He mourns his dead son for several days. His sons and daughters comfort him, but he is beyond comfort. He predicts he will go down to Sheol still mourning[37h]

Meanwhile, the Midianite/Ishmaelites sell Joseph to Potiphar, the captain of Pharaoh's bodyguard.

Genesis 38

Another chapter often passed over for the weekly scripture lesson, Gen. 38 pauses to tell the uplifting story of Tamar and Judah[38a], in which God executes a man for spilling his seed, and Judah has intercourse with his daughter-in-law, more or less by mistake. Another parental advisory has been issued for this chapter.

[KJV 819] TSB 655: *Your Savings 163*

While visiting Hirah, an Adullamite[38b] buddy, Judah meets a Canaanite girl who is identified only as the daughter of Shua. In spite of his family's history of problems with Canaanite wives, he "takes" her and she bears three sons: Er, Onan and Shelah.[38c]

Judah selects a Canaanite woman named Tamar as Er's wife, but Er aggravates God in some unexplained way and God kills him. According to ancient law, Onan (the next brother in line) is required to fulfill his dead brother's husbandly duties.[38d] However, he balks at siring children who won't belong to him, so he ill-advisedly spills his seed on the ground.[38e] Exercising what was evidently a zero tolerance policy on seed wasting, God executes Onan for his deed.

Without commenting directly on the fact that God has killed two of his sons, Judah instructs Tamar to go live with her parents until the third son Shelah is old enough to take over. In an aside, we are told that Judah is somewhat concerned that Shelah is also going to die if he consorts with Tamar.[38f]

After at least a few years, Judah's nameless wife dies. After the mourning period, he and Hirah decide to visit Judah's sheepshearers at Timnah.[38g] Someone mentions to Tamar that Judah is on his way to the sheep shearing hoedown, so she disguises herself in a veil and waits for him at the gateway of a place named Enaim. She is displeased because Shelah has grown up without making her his wife, as Judah promised her after God executed his first two sons.

Judah mistakes her for a harlot, believing from her dress that she is a temple prostitute.[38h] He expresses his interest in having sex with her, and she inquires as to what he is willing to pay. Judah names a kid goat as the price, but indicates he doesn't have one with him. Can he send one over later? Although this is presumably Tamar's first outing as a harlot, she is no fool. She obtains his signet ring, his bracelets[38i] and his staff as a deposit, as it were. When the transaction is complete, she returns home and dresses once again in her widow's clothes.

GENESIS 38 NOTES:

38a. Although this chapter stands on its own as a narrative event, it has significance beyond the sordid little tale that it first appears. Among other things, both King David and Jesus are descended from the illegitimate seed of Tamar and Judah, which has brought about some interesting theology over the years.

38b. The only Adullamite in the Bible.

38c. We are never told her name, although we know Judah's buddy's name.

38d. The Levirate law is from the Latin levir, meaning brother-in-law. Although not specified by God until he dictated the laws to Moses hundreds of years later, the practice was intended to perpetuate the family name and preserve family rights of inheritance in the case of a man who died without male issue.

38e. Now put down your Bible, pick up your dictionary and look up "onanism". That's right.

38f. Shelah has got to be a little nervous at this point.

38g. Timnah is a Canaanite town about 30km northwest of Hebron, where Judah is most likely residing. Hundreds of years in the future, it will be the site of one of Samson's many misadventures.

38h. The temple or cult prostitute concept is challenging for a modern reader. We know historically that "holy" temple servants were a common feature in the religions of Canaan and the ancient Near East and that intercourse was a component in the rites. Furthermore, temple prostitutes were both male and female. The key admonition against homosexuality in Leviticus is believed by many to refer to this scenario because it involved competitive cults.

GENESIS 38 NOTES (continued):

In fact, this practice persisted well into the Third Century A.D. As far as Judah's experience goes, however, it is not certain what "religion" the faux temple prostitute would have belonged to. The Israelites were constantly in trouble with God for embracing the local gods, but did not have a temple of their own until Moses was given painfully detailed instructions during the Exodus. (As we have seen, the Abrahamic family spent a lot of effort on altars and pillars but hadn't built any temples at this point). It is impossible to know what the moral standards of the ancient Israelites and Canaanites really were. However, if an individual "went into" a temple prostitute, it would suggest that he was also an idolater.

38i. The Hebrew word means "cords", which connotes a string decoration for the arms, probably woven in an identifiable pattern as befits his rank.

38j. It is interesting that he inquires around the area for the prostitute, apparently without any sense of embarrassment. Judah's discomfiture has to do with the fact that he was tricked, not that he was out a'whoring.

38k. Zerah means "rising up". Perez means "breach" or "break through".

38l. Tamar is not explicitly described as a Canaanite in the Genesis story, but as a local girl, that is the obvious conclusion. Uncomfortable with this much Canaanite blood in the David-Jesus lineage, many apologists have presented various arguments to the contrary. Directly contradicting those arguments, Tamar is identified in no uncertain terms as a Canaanite in the extended genealogy that opens the book of Chronicles I.

Genesis 38 continued

Judah shows he's a stand up guy by dispatching his pal Hirah with the kid goat in payment for services rendered. The Adullamite naturally can't find the temple prostitute.[38j] "No temple prostitutes been around here," he is told. When Hirah gives Judah the news, Judah comments that he supposes the prostitute will just have to keep his personal items, as he tried in good faith to make payment. But his statement implies that he doesn't want to risk ridicule by conducting a public search for the harlot who duped him.

About three months later, Judah is told by wagging tongues that Tamar is pregnant, obviously the result of harlotry. Demonstrating once again the curious and contradictory moral imperative of his family line, he instructs that she be brought to him so she can be burned for her crime. Tamar instead sends his signet rings and things with the message: *"I am with child by the man to whom these belong."* Oops. Judah decides he might have been a little hasty, and recognizes he is partially to blame for reneging on the Shelah commitment.

To his credit, he does not have sex with his daughter-in-law again. However, he is father to her children, one of whom is an ancestor of both King David and the Christian Messiah.

As it happens, Tamar bears twins, with more of the order-of-birth confusion that seems to run in the family. Zerah appears to be coming out first, so the midwife ties a scarlet thread on his wrist.[38k] But the other newborn soon emerges instead. He is named Perez and he gets only passing mention in the genealogies. This key genealogy is taken up again in Matthew at the very beginning of the New Testament.[38l]

Genesis 39

Returning to the adventures of Joseph, God makes him successful in the house of Potiphar, but the handsome and talented lad gets thrown in jail as the result of spurning the advances of the boss's wife.

[KJV 666] TSB 444: *Your Savings 222*

Once Pharaoh's officer Potiphar sees how the Lord has taken Joseph under his wing, he appoints him as his personal servant and then promotes him overseer of his own household. This good luck rubs off on all of Potiphar's endeavors and he soon leaves all of his affairs to Joseph.[38a]

But as luck would have it, Joseph was a good looking young lad, and Potiphar's wife takes a liking to him. She invites him for some off the clock household tasks, but Joseph turns her down based on his belief that it would be a sin against God. Nevertheless, she keeps working on him and one day grabs him as he comes into the house to do some work. The evil temptress catches him by his robe, which she is left holding as he runs away. Naturally she calls out for help and accuses Joseph of trying to seduce her. She repeats this charge when Potiphar returns home.

Joseph is thrown in jail, where the chief jailer recognizes his potential and places him in charge of all the other prisoners. Some of Joseph's God given mojo rubs off on the chief jailer and he begins to prosper as well.

GENESIS 39 NOTES:

39a. The phrase "concern for nothing but the food he may eat" implies that Potiphar is something of a glutton, which could also explain the perhaps unfulfilled needs of his wife.

40a. Also translated as *"butler"* [KJV].

Genesis 40

Joseph's dream interpretation skills prove useful to Pharaoh's chief cup bearer, but less so for the chief baker.

[KJV 580] TSB 302: *Your Savings 278*

Pharaoh becomes angry with his both his chief cup bearer[40a] and chief baker, and has them incarcerated. Naturally, the chief jailer turns them over to Joseph. After some time, each of the men has vivid dreams, but being in jail, they are dejected because there is no one to interpret the visions. Joseph, understanding that "dreams belong to God", invites the cup bearer and the baker to share with him.

The chief cupbearer's dream involves a vine with three branches. The branches produce blossoms and then clusters of grapes, which the chief cup bearer squeezes into Pharaoh's cup. He places the cup in Pharaoh's hand.

Joseph interprets the dream to mean that Pharaoh will restore the cupbearer to office in three days, at which point he will return to putting the cup in the King's hand. In return for the positive interpretation, Joseph asks him to put in a good word with Pharaoh. He points out that he was kidnapped from the land of the Hebrews in the first place, and has furthermore done nothing wrong here. He was framed.

Encouraged by the happy prediction for his cup bearing colleague, the baker explains his dream. There were three baskets of white bread on his head. In the top basket was baked food for Pharaoh, which was unfortunately being eaten by birds. This time, Joseph's interpretation was less favorable. The dream meant Pharaoh would hang the baker in three days and the birds would eat his flesh.

In three days time, on the occasion of his birthday, Pharaoh declares a feast day for his staff. The day turns out to be more festive for the cup bearer than the baker, as Pharaoh hangs the latter and restores the former to his previous position, as predicted. But the ungrateful cup bearer forgets to get Joseph out of jail.

Genesis 41

Joseph not only interprets Pharaoh's dreams correctly, he goes on to establish some rather visionary agricultural policies.[41a] He becomes governor, gets married, has kids and saves Egypt from a terrible famine.

[KJV 1404] TSB 582: *Your Savings 822*

Two years later, Pharaoh himself has some dreams. As he stands by the river, seven fat cattle come out of the water and graze in the meadow. Then seven lean cattle emerge and eat the fat cattle. He wakes from that dream and has another, in which seven good ears of corn grow on one stalk, followed by seven withered ears that have been "blasted by the east wind."[41b] The seven thin ears devour the seven good ears.

Discomfited by these dreams, Pharaoh calls his magicians to interpret them, but in spite of what seems to be a clear metaphorical message, they all fail. Luckily, the chief cupbearer remembers the assistant jailer, Joseph that Hebrew guy.

Pharaoh summons Joseph, who cleans himself up, changes his clothes and attends the King. Pharaoh tells Joseph he has heard he can do dream interpretation, to which Joseph replies humbly that his power comes from God. But he promises that God will come up with an interpretation favorable to Pharaoh.

Pharaoh repeats both dreams in detail, adding only that the lean cattle did not become fat even after they had eaten the fat cattle. Joseph immediately knows the meaning of the dreams. The seven fat cattle and corn ears represent seven years of prosperity and plenty and the seven thin cattle and withered corn stalks foretell seven years of famine. God is showing Pharaoh what he has planned for the next fourteen years in Egypt. Joseph then repeats the prediction with added drama: God has recapitulated the theme twice due to the grievous nature of the events to come. He wants to make sure Pharaoh gets the message.

Exceeding his dream interpretation mandate, Joseph goes on to provide practical suggestions to the king of Egypt. First, he should appoint a discreet and wise man over Egypt.[41c] Officers under this man would gather and store twenty percent of the grain during the seven plentiful years. The surplus corn would be distributed during the famine years.

This makes total sense to Pharaoh, who rhetorically asks where such a man - a man in whom the spirit of God clearly dwells - might be found? Of course, it is obvious, since God has clued Joseph into the meaning of the dreams, that Pharaoh should appoint Joseph second in command to the boss of Egypt. He takes off his ring, gives it to Joseph, hangs a gold chain around his neck, gets him much nicer threads and lets him ride in the number two chariot. Joseph becomes ruler over Egypt and everyone bows down to him. Best of all, Pharaoh gives him an Egyptian name[41d] and Potipherah the priest's lovely daughter Asenath for a wife.[41e]

At the age of thirty, Joseph does a victory tour of Egypt. During the predicted seven plenteous years, he gathers up the extra grain and stores it in the cities. There is so much that he stops counting it. Also during this time, Joseph's Egyptian wife bears him two sons, Manasseh and Ephraim.[41f]

When the seven years of famine come, they are widespread, affecting the entire region including Canaan. But in Egypt, when the people complain to Pharaoh about the shortages of food, he simply refers them to Joseph. The governor opens the storehouses and sells the surplus crop to the population, as well as to foreigners.[41g]

GENESIS 41 NOTES:

41a. Although there is no evidence at all of a historical Joseph, the Egyptians occasionally appointed foreigners to positions of high authority. An example is the Hyksos Dynasty, pictured in Egyptian art as wearing "cloaks of many colors". They may have been a Semite tribe related to the proto-Israelites.

The Biblical character of Joseph has also been associated with the historical Imhotep, circa 2600 BC. This polymath shares certain characteristics with Joseph, but the time frame is about a thousand years off.

41b. In Exodus 10 and 14, the east wind is summoned by Moses to bring the locusts that plague Egypt and also to part the Red Sea so that the Children of Israel can escape Pharaoh's armies. Several other references associate the east wind with destruction, often of the wicked by God.

41c. Someone, perhaps, who can interpret dreams?

41d. Zaphnathpaaneah. Seriously. The most common interpretation is "revealer of secrets."

41e. Potipherah is the high priest of the god *On*, so Joseph has married into one of the most prominent priestly families in Egypt. *Joseph and Asenath*, a first century A.D. novella, narrates the conversion of Asenath from idolatry to the one true God (El). There is even a magical honeycomb in this legend.

41f. Manasseh is so named because God has made Joseph forget his troubles and his Hebrew family. "Ephraim" means Joseph has been fruitful in the land of his affliction. The boys are half Egyptian, and fathers of half tribes.

41g. But note he is selling their own crops back to them.

GENESIS 42 NOTES:

42a. Benjamin, the youngest, is now Israel's most beloved son, being the other child born to his favorite wife Rachel. A little math, however, tells us that little Benny is in his late-thirties, and, as we will see in Gen. 46, has ten children. Come on Dad. *Please* can I go to Egypt?

42b. It is unclear why getting to slay Reuben's sons would make Israel feel better.

Genesis 42

When Israel's sons go down Egypt to buy grain, Joseph messes with their minds. Holding Simeon as hostage, he sends them back to Hebron to bring his younger brother Benjamin to Egypt.

[KJV 977 TSB 434: *Your Savings 543*

Hearing there is surplus grain in Egypt, Israel tells his sons to stop standing around complaining and go buy some corn. He will not let Benjamin go with the other ten, however, as he is concerned for his safety.[42a]

As governor of Egypt, Joseph is in charge of grain sales, so his brothers find themselves bowing down before him without recognizing him. However, Joseph knows who they are. Recalling his own youthful dreams of the past, he sees that he is still batting a thousand in the dream interpretation department. He decides to have a little payback fun. After grilling them as to their intentions, he accuses them of being spies. In the course of denying the accusation, they tell him the tale of their family, mentioning both their younger brother Benjamin and also their "dead" brother Joseph.

Joseph tells them they will remain as hostages until one of them returns to Canaan and brings back their youngest brother. He puts them in prison for three days, and on the third he relents a bit. He allows all but one to return to Canaan, leaving brother Simeon as hostage until they return with Benjamin. He also lets them take grain back to Canaan to feed the starving. Speaking among themselves in Hebrew, the brothers conclude this is all payback for what they did to Joseph, although they have yet to understand how very karmic it is. Rueben can't resist an "I told you so."

Although Joseph has been speaking to them through an interpreter, he of course understands everything they are saying. He is overcome with emotion, but hides it from them. He has Simeon bound as hostage, but has the sacks of the others filled with grain. He also secretly returns the money to their sacks and sends them on their way.

When they reach an inn, one of the brothers opens his sack to feed his donkey and discovers his money has been returned. As it turns out, all of the brothers' money has been given back. This only makes them all the more paranoid, as they remember the way the governor of Egypt spoke to them, and how they gave him their word they were standup Hebrews.

When they tell Israel what has happened, he is really upset. He begins by lamenting the loss of Joseph, now assuming he has lost Simeon as well. He is extremely reluctant to send Benjamin back to Egypt. Reuben's solution is to tell Israel he is welcome to kill his own two sons if he fails to bring Benjamin home safely.[42b] But Israel is un-persuaded.

Genesis 43

In need of more grain, the hapless brothers head back to see the governor of Egypt, taking Benjamin with them. After some suspense and drama, they have an excellent banquet, with Benjamin getting all the best dishes.

[KJV 938 TSB 393: *Your Savings 545*

The famine continues and Israel's household eats all the previously purchased corn. The Patriarch instructs his sons to return to Egypt for more. Judah reminds his father that the "governor" won't see them unless they bring Benjamin with them. Israel proceeds to blame the whole thing on his sons' poor judgment in telling this governor that they had a brother in the first place.[43a] They do their best to explain that the governor more or less tricked them. Judah reasons with his father and takes responsibility for Benjamin's safety, ultimately pointing out that they could have traveled to Egypt and back in the time it took to argue the point.

Israel then assents, suggesting they take additional presents for the governor, as well as the money that had been placed into their sacks. He waxes resigned to whatever fate may befall his sons. The party leaves (with Benjamin tagging along) and arrives in Egypt. When Joseph sees his brother Benjamin, he instructs his head of household to prepare for a large noon time feast. But the paranoid brothers are afraid, figuring they are being brought to the house because of the money in the sacks. When they arrive at Joseph's place, they attempt to preempt the situation by explaining to the steward how they had found all this money in their sacks, but have now brought it back and so on. The more they explain, the less credible their story sounds.

The steward puts their minds at rest by explaining that it is their particular god whom has given them back their treasure. He returns Simeon, and has his servants give the guys water, wash their feet and feed their donkeys. At the party, the brothers present their gifts and Joseph enquires after their father. He speaks kindly to Benjamin, but is so overcome with emotion that he needs to excuse himself. [43b]

When he returns, Joseph orders lunch served. He eats alone, while the Hebrew brothers also eat separately from the other Egyptians. It is explained matter-of-factly that eating with Hebrews would have been an abomination to the Egyptians. So they sit according to their ages and ranks, and the men "marveled at each other". Joseph sends samples of food from his table, but Benjamin gets five times as much as anyone else.[43c] Nevertheless, they all have a fine party.

GENESIS 43 NOTES:

43a. Neither the brothers nor Israel know the governor is really Joseph. Under normal circumstances, why would the governor of Egypt care about their little brother back in Canaan?

43b. The language in the King James Version *"for his bowels did yearn upon his brother"* [KJV] means at best that he had an upset stomach, and at worst that a more violent intestinal event was taking place. The language is sanitized in most modern translations.

43c. *"Messes from his table"* [KJV] is not a comment on the impeccable Joseph's manners, but rather means a portion served up from a grand banquet table.

GENESIS 44 NOTES:

44a. The magic silver cup is a standard component in similar ancient tales from the region. Egyptians associated such cups with priests and soothsayers, who used silver cups to read signs. This magical thinking was consistent with Joseph's ability to interpret dreams (especially obvious dreams) and also may reflect his marriage into the Egyptian priesthood. Note also that in Egypt, the concept of political and spiritual leadership was intertwined. But if Joseph is dabbling in the occult, is he staying true to his parents' God? As it turns out, Elohim/JHWH already has and will in the future sponsor other magical events. He will also go on to forbid such practices, but He hasn't specifically done so at this point. The pattern is firmly established with Moses: first God encourages magic tricks, then He forbids them (see pro magic instructions in Exodus and strong anti-magic position in Lev. 19-26).

44b. The text describes the group as Judah and his brothers, rather than Reuben and his brothers. We already have reason to believe that Reuben may be more of a lover than junior Patriarch material.

44c. *"God hath found out the iniquity of thy servants."* [KJV] Even though he doesn't know he speaking to Joseph, this statement is commonly taken to mean that judah is vicariously admitting to their guilt in selling Joseph into slavery. He is hinting their bad karma has caught up with them.

44d. The middle aged Benjamin must be a little embarrassed by all this.

Genesis 44

Joseph plays one last scary prank on his brothers.

[KJV 874 TSB 391: *Your Savings 483*

Emotions and digestive tract under control now, Joseph is ready to play one more trick on his brothers. He has his steward place the grain payment money back in the mouths of the sacks, and also has them place his personal silver cup in Benjamin's sack. No sooner have the brothers gone on their way than Joseph sends the steward to apprehend them.

The steward overtakes them and accuses them of stealing Joseph's special cup, the one the governor uses to make prophecies.[44a] The brothers protest that they have previously returned the money they found in their sacks. They suggest that if the steward finds the cup among their baggage, the one who stole it should die and the rest of the family will become the steward's personal slaves. The mellow steward amends the penalty, saying that only the thief will be his slave. For extra drama, the steward conducts his search beginning with Reuben and proceeding in descending age order. Of course, the cup is found in Benjamin's sack.

The Israelite brothers are so upset they tear their clothes. Loading their donkeys they return to the city and find Joseph at his home.[44b] Joseph continues to harass them by hinting he knew what they had done because he is "indeed" a diviner of deeds.

Judah responds in a somewhat curious fashion, declining to deny the theft and admitting to a collective iniquity.[44c] He tells Joseph that he and his brothers are now Joseph's slaves. Joseph declines the offer of all these new slaves and tells Judah that only the guilty one - Benjamin - need stay and be a slave. The rest are free to go in peace to their father.

Flattering Joseph shamelessly, Judah reminds him of a previous conversation in which Joseph insisted that Benjamin come back with his brothers if they expected to see his face again. He recounts their conversation with Israel prior to leaving Canaan, describing his loss of one son already and his extreme reluctance to let the "boy" Benjamin go. Israel's prediction that he will go down to Sheol in sorrow is repeated for Joseph, as is Judah's oath to be surety for Benjamin. Judah begs to be allowed to be Joseph's servant in Benjamin's place. He expresses his fears of the evil that would befall his father if the "lad" doesn't return.[44d]

Genesis 45

Joseph makes himself known to his brothers.

[KJV 731 TSB 372: *Your Savings 359*

At this, Joseph finally cracks and orders everyone out of the room except his brothers. Even so, he begins weeping so loudly the Egyptians hear him, including Pharaoh's household. [45a] He reveals himself to his brothers, who are rendered speechless in amazement and consternation. He gathers them together and tells them that shouldn't be angry with themselves because their evil deed was all part of God's plan to save the family from the famine.[45b] He also points out that there are still five years to go in the down side of the agricultural prophecy.

In other words, it was God who caused them to sell Joseph into slavery, so that he could become Pharaoh's number two guy and boss of all Egypt. He tells his brothers to get back to Canaan, bring back their Dad and get ready to settle in the land of Goshen.[45c] Fetch the whole family and Joseph will provide for everyone, not only during the next five years of famine, but for future generations.[45d] He wants his brothers to hurry and get back to Canaan, so they call tell Dad all about Joseph's splendor in Egypt. Joseph, Benjamin and the other brothers all have a good cry.

When Pharaoh hears Joseph's brothers have come, it pleases him and his servants. He instructs Joseph to tell his brothers to go to Canaan and invite their father and his entire household. Pharaoh promises to settle them on the best land in Egypt. He even gives them wagons to transport the wives and kids. Joseph gives all his brothers new clothes, and, making sure not to learn from his father's mistakes, he bestows an additional three hundred pieces of silver and five new sets of clothes on Benjamin. He sends along donkeys laden with more gifts and food for his Dad.

He packs his brothers off, making sure to tell them not to quarrel on the journey. When they get to Canaan, they break the good news to Israel, who naturally doesn't believe them at first.[45e] But when he sees the Pharaoh's wagons and hears what Joseph has said to his brothers, he believes the story and prepares to visit his long lost son, now governor of Egypt.

GENESIS 45 NOTES:

45a. We don't know how far away Pharaoh's house was from Joseph's.

45b. This time, the Egyptian people are beneficiaries of this far-sited plan, just as they will be collateral damage in the next episode (Exodus). Of course, God could have saved a great deal of effort by not causing the famine in the first place.

45c. Goshen is located in the eastern area of the Nile delta.

45d. As we will see in Exodus, Joseph's ability to predict the future fails him here.

45e. There is no indication here or anywhere else that the brothers take this opportunity to confess their big crime to Israel.

GENESIS 46 NOTES:

46a. At this point there are already several "offering ready" altars at this location.

46b. This is a promise God does not seem to keep, as Israel will die in Egypt and not Canaan. Apologists say that God doesn't promise to bring him back alive, therefore the passage means He will bring his body back to be buried. But the sentence is straightforward and that's not what it says (pull out your copy and read it). Sequentially the text first mentions bringing Israel back, then introduces the topic of death.

46c. One could consider this chapter the first census of Israel.

46d. Joseph should be about 49 during the second year of the famine, and Benjamin is generally understood to be about six years younger than Joseph.

46e. In Acts 7:14, defending himself before the Sanhedrin, Stephen says that 75 people came down to Egypt.

Genesis 46

Israel can't resist stopping off at Beersheba for a few sacrifices, but eventually arrives in Egypt with the whole family. Joseph rides out in triumph to meet them, and to warn them not to mention they are shepherds.

[KJV] 766 TSB 394: *Your Savings 372*

On the way to Egypt, Israel takes the opportunity to stop once more at Beersheba for a last round of sacrifices.[46a] God contacts him in a dream and runs through the eleventh variation of the covenant. He promises to go down to Egypt with Israel and make him the mighty nation he has been promoting since Abraham's days. He guarantees he will bring Israel back to Canaan and assures him that Joseph will be there to close his eyes when he dies.[46b]

Off they go to Egypt, Israel, his wives, children, grandchildren, livestock and other property.

We are going to save a lot of time again by not listing all of Israel's family: his sons and their first generation of descendants.[46c] However, there are some essential points buried in this genealogy. First, when Judah's offspring are listed, Er and Onan are said to have "died" in the land of Canaan (Gen38). Shelah, who was originally promised to Tamar as a replacement, is not mentioned (but will appear in the genealogy in *Chronicles*). The only two children of Judah itemized in Genesis are Perez and Zerah, the twin result of the illicit coupling with his Canaanite daughter-in-law. Further genealogies will reveal that both King David and Jesus are descended from Judah / Tamar / Perez. For fun, recall from Gen. 9 that Noah placed a curse on Ham's son Canaan's descendants for his crime of looking at Noah's drunken naked body. Therefore, both King David and the Messiah carry the curse of Ham.

Rachel's offspring are numbered at fourteen, including Joseph, Benjamin, Benjamin's ten sons and Joseph's two sons by his Egyptian wife. We know the name of Joseph's wife, but Benjamin's wife (or wives) is never mentioned.[46d]

According to Genesis, the total number of Israel's household was seventy people.[46e] The percentage of the early descendants of Israel with Egyptian, Canaanite and slave blood is very high.

As the host arrives in Goshen, Joseph rides out to meet them in his chariot. He and his father have an emotional embrace. Curiously, after all these years, what seems to be uppermost in Joseph's thoughts is to warn his family not to tell Pharaoh they are shepherds. Instead, they are to tell Pharaoh they are keepers of livestock. As the text explains: *"for every shepherd is loathsome to the Egyptians."* [KJV]

Genesis 47

Pharaoh settles Israel's clan on prime land while Joseph bamboozles the entire population of Egypt out of everything they own, allowing them to become slaves on their own land. Israel prepares for an extended dying process.

[KJV 965] TSB 503: *Your Savings 462*

Joseph chooses five unidentified brothers to go meet Pharaoh, but not necessarily the five smartest. Sure enough, the first thing Pharaoh inquires about is what type of work the Israelites do. In spite of Joseph's previous warning, the brothers immediately tell Pharaoh they are shepherds.[47a] Fortunately, Pharaoh appears to pass over this critical livestock management nomenclature issue. He graciously grants Egypt's best lands to Israel's offspring and offers the competent family members employment managing his royal cattle.

Israel is then introduced to Pharaoh, who asks him how old he is. After giving his age as one-hundred thirty, Israel goes on to describe his years as "few and unpleasant". He further complains that he hasn't lived as long as his forefathers did.[47b] Following this whine fest, Israel blesses Pharaoh and takes his leave. Joseph settles the family in the land of Rameses and provides them with food.[47c]

However, he doesn't treat the Egyptians quite as well. With the famine increasingly severe, he collects all the money in Egypt from the starving people in order to sell them back the grain he appropriated from them during the seven years of plenty. Joseph takes the cash to Pharaoh. When the people's money is all spent, he demands all the livestock in Egypt as payment for the next year's food. Once that food is gone, the people beg Joseph to purchase their land and buy them as slaves to work their former fields. Joseph agrees to the deal, and provides them with seeds.[47d] Now owning all the land of Egypt on behalf of the King, Joseph rather matter-of-factly goes about establishing a feudal society that would make a Middle Ages baron blush. He relocates the people from one end of the country to the other as he sees fit. The exception is the priests, which live off an allotment from Pharaoh.

Joseph delivers seed and graciously allows the people to begin planting on the land they previously owned. He informs them that they are permitted to keep four fifths of the harvest, with one fifth going to Pharaoh. Such as mensch, this man.

Having lost everything to a system that forces them to give up everything they own for the privilege of buying back their own food, the people jubilantly celebrate Joseph's generosity in saving their lives. *"And they said, Thou hast saved our lives: let us find grace in the sight of my lord, and we will be Pharaoh's servants."* [KJV] This would make any reasonable person happy.

Meanwhile, Israel's clan settles in Goshen, acquiring property and being fruitful. Despite his previous complaints, Israel in fact lives on for another seventeen years after his premature pre-death diatribe. Nevertheless, at the age of one hundred forty-seven, the time comes for him to die. He calls Joseph and has him swear with his hand under his thigh that the governor will not bury him in Egypt. Joseph swears that he will bury his father at the traditional family tomb, and Israel bows his head in worship.

GENESIS 47 NOTES:

47a. Why the brothers decide to tell him they are shepherds is anyone's guess. It clearly doesn't matter to Pharaoh one way or the other, so either Joseph was being paranoid, or there is a redaction disconnect.

47b. Since he doesn't yet know how long he is going to live, and has just been given a major gift by the king of Egypt, one can't help but feel the Patriarch is being ungracious.

47c. Rameses (Tell el-Daba) is one of the towns in the Goshen area on the eastern side of the Pelusiac branch of the Niles. Rameses is the starting point of the forty year Exodus journey.

47d. *"…And give [us] seed, that we may live, and not die, that the land be not desolate."* [KJV] Although none of this can be proven, detailed Egyptian records show that from the Middle Kingdom on everything already belonged to Pharaoh.

If we accept internal Bible time accounting, then Joseph's rule would have to fall in what is termed Egypt's "Second Intermediate Period", between the Middle and New Kingdoms, or about 1786-1570 BC. In non-biblical history, an Asiatic group called the Hyksos ruled the delta of the Nile during this period. The Egyptians would have regarded the Israelites as "Asiatic". It is tricky to reconcile internal Biblical timelines with what we know of history, especially this far in the past. However, this is almost the only way we can keep the Bible on a realistic track that reconciles its own internal timeline and historical timelines. In the Bible narrative, the Exodus takes place anywhere from 150 to 430 years after Joseph dies.

GENESIS 48 NOTES:

48a. This was the scene of Jacob/Israel's dream on the rock pillow regarding the ladder to heaven.

48b. For purposes of inheritance, this is not an empty gesture. In effect, this act diverts Reuben's birthright as punishment for his wicked ways. The double portion, which would traditionally have gone to Reuben as the eldest son, is now given to Joseph's children. This is the origin of a math anomaly that troubles casual Bible readers, because it seems to establish thirteen tribes, rather than the twelve of common lore. Although the tribal structure of Israel is based on the twelve sons of Jacob/Israel, there are indeed thirteen tribes in all. When the various tribes eventually receive their land inheritance in the Promised Land (Joshua chapters 13-19), there is no "Joseph" tribe. Instead, "the sons of Joseph," Manasseh and Ephraim are counted as distinct tribes in Israel. We will see that the tribe of Levi is not given land and doesn't count in the territorial mapping of greater Israel. So there are twelve tribal regions in Canaan / Palestine, but thirteen total tribes.

48c. Considered by many to be Bethlehem.

Genesis 48

Another deathbed scene for Israel combining poignancy, slapstick and important business communications. Israel claims Manasseh and Ephraim as his children, then seats the twenty-something boys on his lap to bestow his Patriarchal blessing on the wrong twin on purpose.

[KJV 619 TSB 482: *Your Savings 137*

Having exacted Joseph's promise, Israel continues living for an unspecified period. Eventually however, Joseph is summoned again to his father's deathbed and this time the situation seems serious enough that he brings his two half-Egyptian sons, Manasseh and Ephraim. With great effort, Israel sits up in bed and divulges his previous discussion with God at Luz.[48a] He repeats an abridged version of the covenant and the land grant for the twelfth time in Genesis.

Israel then promotes Manasseh and Ephraim to the same inheritance level as Reuben and Simeon. [48b] The dying Patriarch rambles a bit about Rachel dying in Canaan and burying her in Ephrath[48c], then asks to see Manasseh and Ephraim in order to bless them.

Seating the pair of twenty-something tykes on his lap, Israel re-blesses them and indicates once again they will be equal to their uncles when the estate is divided up.

Although they have been sitting on his knees in the previous passage and he has just included them twice in his inheritance, the partially blind and apparently senile Israel now asks Joseph who these two boys are. Joseph "brings them close" (although they are already on his knees) and Israel kisses them. Israel remarks that he never expected to see Joseph again, and now he has been able to see his children.

The next scene clearly references a major blessing mix up event from Israel's distant past but his time with Israel in the role of Patriarch. While the outcome is similar, this time Israel switches blessings on purpose.

When it comes time for the formal blessing, Joseph positions the twins according to their age, which is to say, Ephraim (the younger) near Israel's left hand and Manasseh (the elder) near his right. But Israel purposefully switches his hands and gives the younger brother the right hand blessing.

Genesis 48 continued

His blessing message repeats the familiar covenant references about breeding into a great multitude, and reaffirms the close association between Abraham, Isaac and their personal God. At this point, Joseph notices that his blind Dad is messing up the blessing assignments and attempts to switch Israel's hands to the proper twin, but Israel tells him he knows what he is doing.[48d] In the peculiar way this family has about casually pronouncing long term personal prophecies, Israel reveals that Ephraim is going to be greater than Manasseh, and that his descendants will be an entirely different multitude of nations.[48e]

Israel again informs Joseph he is about to die, but not to worry because God will take Joseph back to the land of his fathers.[48f] He also adds to Joseph's inheritance portion[48g] by granting a semantically tricky gift: a specific piece of land near Shechem. Israel makes reference to having taken this "portion"[48h] from the Amorites by his sword. But there is no record of Israel taking *anything* from any Amorites, or even drawing his sword for that matter.

GENESIS 48 NOTES (continued):

48d. Israel's eyes are described as dim from age, but compared to the life spans of previous generations, he's still a young buck.

48e. Have a nice day, Manasseh! Joshua, for one, is of the tribe of Ephraim.

48f. *"But God shall be with you, and bring you again unto the land of your fathers."* [KJV] Israel doesn't mention that Joseph will be dead four hundred years before God brings him in the form of an Egyptian mummy back to the land of his fathers. Without jumping into this particular scholarly debate, we are content to examine the Biblical text at face value and conclude that God probably didn't break the promise Israel made on his behalf, but rather, the rambling Israel was characteristically obtuse in his language.

48g. As the number two guy in the incredibly wealthy land of Egypt, Joseph's need of Israel's inheritance is probably minimal.

48h. We have seen that Shechem is the name of both the city of the massacre in Gen.34 and Hamor's amorous son Shechem, the prince of the same city. In this reference, the word used for the portion given to Joseph is also Shechem, meaning "shoulder". In the book of Joshua, the tribe of Manassah does end up with a land allotment that includes the city of Shechem.

GENESIS 49 NOTES:

49a. This is the resolution to what seemed to be a throwaway interlude in Genesis 35, when we heard in passing that Reuben has been overly friendly with Bilhah. At that point, there is no mention of Israel's reaction. It is typical of many of these interludes that they are suddenly resolved many chapters, or in some cases books, later. So it turns out that Israel has been fuming all this time and has been writing a poem as therapy.

49b. In spite of this apparent moral failing, Levi's offspring will be selected as the priestly class.

49c. This prophecy projects us ahead to the assignments of land for the various tribes in the book of Joshua. Simeon's tract is literally surrounded by Judah's in the southern part of the Promised Land.

49d. Shiloh is a Hebrew word meaning "He Whose It Is," or "He to Whom It Belongs." This is often taken to be an early prophecy of the coming of Jesus, who is descended from Judah. Shiloh is used in the Talmud (an encyclopedia of post biblical Jewish tradition) as a personal name for the Messiah. So the exact identity of Shiloh depends on the interpreter. Some writers also view the incident it as a foreshadowing of King David.

49e. Doesn't turn out that way - Manasseh, Asher and Dan get the waterfront locations.

49f. The tribe of Dan (son of Bilhah) is represented by scales because the word "dan" means judgment. Dan and his tribe are also indicated by a snake or serpent because of references in this chapter.

Genesis 49

Continuing on his deathbed, Israel performs a prophetic poem that is better news for some sons than for others. The mysterious Shiloh is mentioned for the only time. Then Israel dies.

[KJV 766] TS 531: *Your Savings 235*

Israel assembles his sons and recites a sort of freeform poem describing their inheritance and prophesizing their futures. Some are encouraging, others less so, and still others are somewhat hazy.

Reuben has dignity and power, but at the same time is as uncontrolled as water. Israel deprives him of his birthright (which he has already done in effect in the previous chapter) because of his bad habit of sleeping with Dad's concubine (Bilhah).[49a]

Simeon and Levi are castigated for their massacre of innocent, recently circumcised men in Shechem. [49b] Israel notes that in their anger they not only slew men, but they also lamed oxen. He curses their anger and promises to disperse them in Israel.[49c]

Judah is described with a great deal of lion-based metaphor. Not only will his hand be on the neck of his enemies, but his brothers will also bow down to him. This will require an attitude adjustment, as they are currently bowing down to Joseph. As a ruler, Judah will prevail until a previously unmentioned individual named Shiloh comes.[49d] There is some additional wine-related imagery, which includes the line: *"His eyes [shall be] red with wine, and his teeth white with milk."* [KJV]

In Zebulon's brief mention, Israel predicts he will dwell at the seashore and be a haven for ships. [49e]

Issachar is described as a "strong donkey" who decides on a good resting place, but becomes a slave at forced labor.

Dan's prediction is as overwrought as it is confusing. He is portrayed first as a judge over his people (because his name means judgment), then as a serpent, then as a horned snake that bites a horse's heels and causes the rider to fall backwards.[49f]

Genesis 49 continued

Possibly stalling for time, Israel inserts a quick request to God (*"For Your salvation I wait, O LORD"*) and then continues the prophecy poem.

Gad will be "raided by raiders" but he will also raid them.[49g] By contrast, Gad's full brother Asher will have rich food and produce royal dainties.

Napthali also gets two cryptic lines: he is a doe let loose and he brings forth beautiful words. [49h]

Joseph, naturally, gets the full treatment. In Israel's accounting, Pharaoh's governor begins as a fruitful bough by a spring, with its branches running over a wall, then for undisclosed reasons, archers attack and harass him. His arms are agile and the bow is firm, due to what seems to be a transmission of strength from God (the Mighty One of Jacob, the Shepherd, the Stone of Israel).

Israel outlines a series of blessing sources, including some from the heavens above and some from the deep. If that isn't enough, he throws in blessings of the breasts and of the womb. He points out one more time that Joseph is distinguished among his brothers.

His little brother Benjamin is characterized as a ravenous wolf, devouring prey in the morning and dividing the spoil in the evening.[49i] Who knew?

The conclusion of the blessing poem notes that the citations are appropriate for each brother, but the narrative doesn't register their reactions to Israel's frank assessment of their abilities and prospects.

Israel asks to be buried at Macpelah and then dies. He is "gathered to his people".

GENESIS 49 NOTES (continued):

49g. Gad, which means "soldier" or "luck", is a son of Leah's slave Zilpah. The mention of raiding probably refers to the tribe's location on the northeastern border of the Northern Kingdom (Judges).

49h. *"Naphtali is a hind let loose: he giveth goodly words."* [KJV] In modern times, Israeli tribal flags include a depiction of a doe or hind. The best interpretation of Napthali's persona is that he was something of a metro sexual.

49i. This description of Benjamin is a far cry from the little guy Israel won't allow to go down to Egypt with his brothers.

GENESIS 50 NOTES:

Date: ~ 1675 B.C.

50a. The embalmment / mummification of Israel and later Joseph comprise the only references to this proprietary Egyptian burial ritual found in the Bible. The expensive and exclusive honor is clearly granted because Joseph is a high Egyptian official. Embalming was a key component in the mythologically complex Egyptian vision of the afterlife, and therefore a curious choice for a non-idolator such as Joseph. Many other factors in the Joseph story make us wonder how committed to the Elohim/JHWH lifestyle he was. Modern Jewish law rules that embalming is forbidden unless the body is being transported over state lines, in which case it is permitted.

50b. About forty years shorter. And if the Israelites had only remained in Canaan after the funeral - the land that God has promised them thirteen times - a lot of trouble (plagues, drowned charioteers, dead Egyptian children etc.) could have been avoided.

50c. Joseph tells Pharaoh that Israel wanted to be buried "in my grave which I dug for myself in the land of Canaan", but most analysts assume that he must mean the Cave of the Patriarchs originally purchased from the Hittites. In any case, he was buried at Machpelah. Remember, Isaac also claimed to have taken land from Amorites with his sword.

50d. The name of the threshing floor means "bramble" or "thorn" and would most likely have been associated with a great farmer or regional chief. It would have been in the open air and able to accommodate the large mourning party. It was common to make a hedge fence of brambles around a threshing floor.

50e. Abel-mizraim = the "meadow of Egypt".

50f. The assumption being that Israel had been protecting them, but the previous events don't support this. Joseph had them at his mercy several times.

Genesis 50

Israel gets mummified and taken back to the family burial cave by an entourage of Hebrews and senior Egyptians. Joseph also dies and gets mummified.

[KJV 687] TSB 409: *Your Savings 278*

After some conspicuous lamentation, Joseph has his physicians embalm his father.[50a] In other words, Israel becomes a mummy. This requires forty days, and the Egyptians weep a total of seventy days for Israel. Joseph gets permission from Pharaoh to take Israel back to Hebron for burial and even gets Pharaoh's servants and - unbelievably - all the elders of Egypt to go with him. When you add in Joseph's whole family, horsemen, chariots and so on, it must have been a huge assemblage of people traveling to Canaan to pay their last respects to Israel. Conceptually, we might think of it as a trial run for the Exodus in four hundred years, except this time Egyptians peacefully accompany the Israelites and the trip is considerably less time consuming.[50b]

Once in Canaan, instead of going to Machpelah[50c], the burial party goes instead to the threshing floor of Atad for an additional seven days of a very great and sorrowful lamentation.[50d] When the Canaanites see this gathering, they conclude that it is an Egyptian funeral, and name the place Abel-mizraim.[50e]

After the mourning event, Israel's sons make their way to Machpelah and bury him there. They return to Egypt. With Israel dead, Joseph's other brothers (probably with the exception of Benjamin) become paranoid, imagining Joseph is now going to take revenge for their misdeeds. They send a message to Joseph fabricating a statement from Israel, saying that just before he died, he definitely commanded that Joseph should forgive their transgressions from at least thirty years previously.

This makes Joseph cry and his brothers come and prostrate themselves. Joseph speaks kindly to them and reminds them that he does not presume to act in God's place. He explains again that even though they meant evil against him, God actually engineered their crime in order to set the table for all the good things that had now come to pass.[50f] He re-affirms that he will provide for them. Joseph lives to one hundred ten, able to see many generations of his children grow up. As he prepares to die, he once more reassures his brothers that God will take over in terms of seeing after their well being. He makes his brothers promise to carry his body back to Canaan. He is also embalmed, mummified and placed in a coffin. The professional embalming will prove to be prescient, as Joseph's body won't be returned to the oft promised land for four more centuries.